● ● ●

Imago Dei® Psychotherapy:
A Catholic Conceptualization

G. C. Dilsaver, MTS, PsyD

Sapientia Press
of Ave Maria University

In Dedication

To my parents for providing the foundation
To my wife for providing the love
To Nuestra Señora de Guadalupe for simply providing

Imago Dei

Requests for permission to make copies of any part of the work should be directed to:

Sapientia Press
of Ave Maria University
5050 Ave Maria Blvd.
Ave Maria, FL 34142
888-343-8607

Cover Design: Eloise Anagnost

Cover Image: Courtesy of Divinity and Religious Studies, University of Aberdeen, from an original design by Christine Mackenzie. Copyright remains with the School of Divinity, History and Philosophy, University of Aberdeen.

Printed in the United States of America.

Library of Congress Control Number: 2007926233

ISBN-13: 978-1-932589-40-5

Table of Contents

Foreword

THERAPEUTIC undertakings, whether in medicine or in psychology, proceed from assumptions that are necessary if the very concept of "therapy" is to be intelligible. In medicine, which is the beneficiary of cumulative information drawn from both the laboratory and the clinic, there is a broadly settled position on the signs and significance of pathological processes and treatment modalities likely to be successful. This very settled position, however, is itself grounded in assumptions about normal physiological processes and the degree to which departures from the norm finally qualify as pathological. Briefly put, medical treatments begin where the patient no longer matches up with the model or theory of the healthy body.

Psychotherapy, too, is intelligible as an undertaking only insofar as there is a model or theory of the healthy person—the healthy mental life—not sufficiently reflected in the life of this person, this patient. It is therefore something of a professional self-delusion for therapists to insist that they are "neutral" on the question of the nature of human nature and (therefore) the conditions favoring its flourishing. Therapy begins with a theory or conception of—Dare I say it?—*the right life*, no matter how widely placed are the perimeters.

In *Imago Dei Psychotherapy* Dr. Dilsaver comes to grips with this unavoidable starting point and defends a conception of human nature that he would have guide therapeutic practice. The foundation he builds is, as he says, "intrinsically dependent on a Catholic philosophy and theology" (p. 11). He finds within the doctrinal teaching of the Church, developed over two millennia, a systematic anthropology able to comprehend the fullest range of human values and human interests. The teaching is *essentialist* and thus is assuredly not confined to Roman Catholics. Indeed, the (Thomistic) essentialism that is integral to this anthropology "does not require the overt inclusion of faith principles" (p. 135) within the therapeutic context. What is advanced is a conception of human nature with which to understand the troubled and incomplete life and then the elements that must be incorporated into this life to relieve it and permit it to begin the process of redeeming its fuller and fullest promise.

In a manner redolent of Kant's suspension of reason in order to leave room for faith, Dr. Dilsaver concludes that it is only Faith that "allows man to transcend the limits of his intellect" (p. 145). In this he shares the general view of clinicians: Intellectualizing one's condition is unlikely to reach its core, its consequences, and the means by which to change it. Does this amount to little more than a defense of "pastoral counseling"? The answer will depend on the extent to which the "pastor" is in possession of a coherent, robust, faithful-to-the-facts, and systematic psychology. The argument of *Imago Dei Psychotherapy* is that Roman Catholic teaching can provide this and that alternatives, to the extent that they depart from this teaching, cannot. What makes this such an important book is that it thus invites reflection and criticism. It is a book that actually takes a position—and on nothing less than human nature and its prospects.

—Daniel N. Robinson
Philosophy Faculty
Oxford University

Introduction

THE NEED for the development of a Catholic clinical psychology is urgent. Not only are confessors hard pressed to find Catholic clinicians for penitents who manifest psychological needs beyond their clerical competency and responsibility, but the profession of psychology itself would profit immensely by accessing the wellsprings of truth concerning the human person that are found in the Catholic worldview. In practice, the Catholic clinical psychology herein espoused need not be *overtly* Catholic, for its implementation entails philosophical principles once removed from the Catholic theological truths that have facilitated their elucidation.

One would expect that, given the academic and humanistic tradition of Catholicism and the fact that the very matrix of modern science itself is the Catholic Christendom of the Middle Ages, Catholic clinical psychology would be a well-established and defined entity; however, because of historical and spiritual factors (outlined in subsequent chapters) this has not been the case. In fact, amazingly, the *Imago Dei Psychotherapy (IDP)* conceptualization presented in this treatise comes on the scene as the seminal school of a belated Catholic clinical psychology.

Because of this seminal nature, the foundational principles identified herein are expected to be in some way integral to any subsequent psychotherapy that is truly Catholic. Although these principles could be subject to categorization, emphasis, expression, and application in various combinations by other theoreticians, they may be nonetheless considered essential constants of a Catholic clinical psychology, being derived as they are from the Church's theological and philosophical understanding of the human person.

The teleological, epistemological, and moral teachings of the Church in her presentation of an adequate anthropology are of utmost import for such a conceptualization. The validation of any particular Catholic qua Catholic clinical psychology, including that of IDP, will be determined by how fully it adheres to and applies the Church's understanding of the human person.

Imago Dei Psychotherapy specifically adheres to and applies the Catholic worldview in a Thomistically-based and existentially-orientated manner. IDP's Thomistic base best assures its orthodox moorings, which provide the clinician with the objective and normative truths concerning the human person that are necessary for the restoration of mental health. Imago Dei Psychotherapy's existential orientation, itself derived from the Thomistic philosophy of existence or being, gives primacy to the person's transcendental yearnings as a *seeker of truth* and allows the clinician to enter into the subjectivity of a therapant[1] and thus appraise his mental state.

As the name implies, Imago Dei Psychotherapy seeks to restore the image of God when that image (i.e., the rational/volitional nature of the human person) is marred by mental illness and personality distortions. Imago Dei Psychotherapy conceptualizes restoring the image of God, or the regaining of mental health, as enabling a therapant *to perceive, receive, reflect upon, and act upon the real.* This Imago Dei psychotherapeutic conceptualization is based on the Thomistic principle of moral agency which holds that the fully human act entails rational assent to truth and a subsequent volitional embracing of this truth as the good.

This treatise aims at facilitating the establishment of a clinical practice that is integrally located within an orthodox Catholic worldview, taking as its end that which the Church holds out to be the good of the person: a good that is, finally, of the soul, and thus entails the *sanctification of the person.* At the same time, IDP recognizes that whereas the Church is concerned specifically with sanctification, and hence with the remission of sin and the transmission of grace, Catholic psychology qua psychology is concerned specifically with mental health.

The *eradication* of sin and the *implementation* of grace are outside the realm of psychology's competency; however, the *effects* of sin and grace are

---

[1] The term *therapant*, or a person who is receiving psychotherapy, is herein introduced to avoid the consumeristic connotation of "client," the passive connotation of "patient," and the confessorial connotation of "directee."

of utmost clinical concern. Whereas the sacraments deal with the eradication of sin, psychotherapy deals with the eradication of sin's effects, be these the residual effects of original sin (dimming of the intellect, weakening of the will, and concupiscence) or actual sin (acquired characterological flaws). So too, while the sacraments and grace can directly impact the efficacy of the therapeutic process, psychology can indirectly impact sanctification by removing obstacles that impede receptiveness to God's grace. Indeed, psychotherapeutic change is at times necessary before a person can effectively enter into spiritual direction.

While new scientific techniques are expected to be produced by Catholic clinical psychology, nonetheless, it is not the science of psychology that is essentially distinctive in such a clinical practice, but rather the ordering and locating of that science within the Catholic worldview. When this is done, not only is the faith of the therapant facilitated or nurtured, but—and this is the driving hypothesis of this treatise—*the potential of clinical psychology is actualized in a superlative manner when it avails itself of the fullness of truth concerning the person that only the Church possesses.* An authentic Catholic clinical psychology, then, entails both a scientific psychology that depends on the truths of philosophical psychology and a philosophical psychology that is validated by and draws on sacred theology.

The complete propriety of such a subalternated[2] position of psychology to Catholicism via philosophy is a singular phenomenon, for Catholicism is singular as a religion in its thorough and correct philosophical enunciation. As such, this treatise utilizes a paradigm of integration not apparent in modern integrative literature, which has historically been developed from a Protestant point of view. The model of subalternation employed herein works best with a worldview that has a comprehensive, integral, and definitive metaphysics that is able to subsume fully and directly the science of psychology. The dearth of philosophical augmentation in the Evangelicalism from which much of the integrative efforts have arisen and the inherent lack of unified thought in the varied worldviews of Protestantism have made such a subalternation unattainable from the Protestant perspective. So too, the historic divorce in Protestantism of grace and nature,

---

[2] In Scholasticism, the direct dependence of a lower science upon the truths of a higher science is termed *subalternation.* See chapter 2, "Subalternating Psychology to Catholic Truth."

and therefore, faith and reason, makes its integration altogether different from a Catholic integration.

Because Imago Dei Psychotherapy is based directly on the philosophical truths of Catholicism/Thomism and is therefore one step removed from theology, it need not employ revealed truths in its therapy or require faith from its therapants. The nature of the human person remains the same regardless of their belief system. However, a practicing IDP clinician's expertise and efficacy is greatly impacted by his intellectual assent and moral conformation to the Catholic worldview. The more a clinician is himself able to convert and conform to reality and to Christ (and Him crucified) the more he is able to guide therapants, who themselves must courageously engage this reality in an intensive and arduous process that requires nothing less than a "dying to self."

Most of the founders of modern psychology had an aversion to the absolutism of the God of Revelation and subsequently to the absolutism of Catholicism. One of these founders was William James (1842–1910), the father of the psychology of religion and the darling of many Protestant integrators because of his openness to an indefinite (but definitely not Catholic) spirituality. In his seminal work *Varieties of Religious Experience*, James sardonically writes, "[I]f we could descend on our subject from above like Catholic theologians, with our fixed definitions of man and man's perfection and our positive dogmas about God, we should have an easy time of it" (Lecture XIV).

James was inadvertently prophetic. There has been, and it is expected there will continue to be, a certain ease and facility that accompanies the belated development of Catholic clinical psychology—since truth begets truth. Such has been the case with the development of Imago Dei Psychotherapy, a gift from the treasury of the Church that required relatively minimal innovation in its theoretical formulation. Finally, remarkable clinical outcomes already promise that the implementation of a Catholic clinical psychology subalternated to Catholicism's "fixed definitions" and "positive dogmas" will in time yield a substantial body of empirical evidence that will irrefutably witness to such a psychology's superior therapeutic efficacy, thus adding another confirmation that these Catholic definitions and dogmas truly do descend from above.

● ● ●

CHAPTER 1

Modern Origins and Trends of Catholic Psychology

CLINICAL PSYCHOLOGY developed from experimental or laboratory psychology, work that sought to study mental phenomena rather than to heal mental illness. Before examining the history and literature of a specifically Catholic clinical psychology, it is therefore necessary to look at its foundation in Catholic experimental psychology.

In Germany, Johannes Müller (1801–1858) was the father of experimental physiology and physiological psychology. In particular Müller's *Handbuch der Physiologie des Menschen für Verkesungen* (1834) first wedded physiology to psychology. Müller found his physiological empiricism compatible with, indeed facilitated by, Thomistic and Catholic principles, for the father of experimental physiology was also a staunch proponent of hylomorphism, or the soul/body composite of man. Indeed, Müller's Catholic faith was the impetus of his scientific research. Upon his death, Muller's national obituary read:

> Unspoiled by the glory and renown which were his he never wavered for a moment from his firm and humble faith of his boyhood; in public and private he was the most religious of men, and the deeper he pierced into the secrets of science, the more ardently he cried out in praise of the wisdom and greatness of God. (As quoted in Misiak and Staudt 1954, 21)

Müller's disciples include such towering figures as Wilhelm Wundt (1832–1920), the father of experimental psychology, and Herman Von

Helmholtz (1821–1894),[1] the author of the conservation of energy theory. Wundt would hold, like his mentor Müller, that psychology is inseparable from philosophy.

Another Catholic, Desiré Cardinal Mercier (1851–1926) advanced the science of experimental psychology in Belgium. While at Louvain University, Mercier would view experimental psychology as an auxiliary or subalternated science to rational psychology, integrating it with Thomism. Mercier's *Les Origines de la psychologie contemporaine* (1897) was a history of psychology as well as an application of Thomism to the current state of psychology. Mercier would continually warn of the dangers of materialistic monism, psychology cut adrift from a solid philosophy such as Thomism.

Initially it appeared that psychology might well grow to maturation in integral relation with the philosophical matrix from which it sprang. It is natural that the Catholic philosophers who branched into and pioneered experimental psychology would do so from a Thomistic metaphysical position.[2] Such a movement was facilitated when Leo XIII (1810–1903) issued his encyclical *Aeterni Patris* (1879), officially launching the neo-Thomistic movement the same year Wundt opened the psychological laboratory initiating experimental psychology. Three decades later, the Catholic academic world again received magisterial instruction when St. Pius X (1835–1914) issued his prophetic *Lamentabili Sane* (1907) and *Pascendi Dominici Gregis* (1907), exhorting the faithful to maintain Catholic truths in the face of a waxing secularism, the theological and philosophical errors of which were delineated and labeled "modernism."

---

[1] Freud took his "psychic energy model" from Helmholtzian physics, which included the theory of the conservation of energy.

[2] Among the more prominent early experimental Catholic psychologists (all priests) who sought such an integration were the Irish Jesuit Michael Maher (1860–1918), who in *Psychology: Empirical and Rational* (1890) maintained that philosophical and experimental psychology are inseparable, because science must needs locate itself within a metaphysical construct (a position echoed a century later by non-Catholics Browning [1987] and O'Donohue [1989]); Armand Thiéry (1868–1932), a prodigy of Mercier's who studied under Wundt; Johannes Lindworsky, S.J. (1875–1939), whose main contribution was in volitional psychology and motive formation in will training; and Émile Peillaube (1864–1934), a proponent of Thomistically based psychology and thus hylomorphism. In addition, though most secular and Protestant psychologists desired to sever the ties between psychology and philosophy, founding psychologists of the stature of Wundt and William James (1842–1910) advocated a philosophically-informed psychology.

The presence of a growing number of Catholics in the field of psychology, combined with the resurgence of a vigorous Thomism and the Church's concise and sure guidance against secularism, boded well for the full development of an authentically Catholic experimental and, eventually, clinical psychology in the twentieth century. Tragically, the promise of Catholic psychology would remain unfulfilled, as would the short-term measurable promise of the Church herself.[3] The Church, having weathered the revolutions, persecutions, and Kulturkampf of the recent centuries (symbolically culminated in the loss of the ancient Papal States), experienced in the first half of the century a growing and unmatched moral influence in the world and a deluge of converts and vocations within her ranks. Tragically, two world wars and their subsequent social and moral upheaval would advance secularism in spite of Catholic efforts to the contrary.

Nowhere is the abdication of this Catholic promise more clear-cut and harmful than in the area of psychology. Even in the beginning, the presence of prominent and staunchly Catholic experimental psychologists was matched by the presence of many who strayed from the faith. These included Franz Brentano (1838–1917), a former priest, former Catholic, and one-time teacher of Freud, who seemed destined to be the father of modern Catholic psychology,[4] both scientific and Thomistic, before his precipitous fall from grace; Carl Stumpf (1848–1936), Brentano's disciple and fellow apostate, who cofounded with Brentano the school of functionalism; and August Messer (1867–1937) and Karl Marbe (1869–1953),

---

3 The grim statistical data—be it in the decimation of the priestly and religious vocations, the closing of Catholic schools, or the adherence of Catholics to Church teachings and prescriptions—indicates that what promised to be a golden era for the Church has become instead a time of devastation of arguably unprecedented proportions. According to *The Pew Forum on Religion and Public Life* (2008) in a report, titled *U.S. Religious Landscape Survey*, roughly one-third of United States respondents who were raised in the Church say they no longer identify themselves as Catholic. One must also wonder about the quality of the Catholicism of the remaining two-thirds that still claim Catholic affiliation when other polls have shown that roughly ninety percent dissent on grave Church teachings.

4 Brentano did end up being the father of functional psychology, which views behavior in terms of active adaptation to the environment. As such, in functional psychology's extreme form, as developed by Dewey, the good or true is synonymous with "whatever works." This functionalism is the basis today for the profession of psychology's definition of mental health (see in chapter 3, "The Teleology of Secularism").

both founding members of the influential Würzburg school[5] of German psychology, and both apostates. These and other less prominent defections from the ranks of psychology throughout the last century should raise grave concerns about the spirit of an empirical science, and an experimental psychology in particular, that claims autonomy from philosophical and theological truths.

In distinction from those who eschewed a Catholic philosophical basis of psychology, there remained many Catholic psychological experimentalists who held with varying degrees of conviction that philosophical positions should in some way influence psychology. Such advocates included the Jesuit Joseph Fröbes (1866–1947), a disciple of Müller; the diocesan priest Edward Pace (1861–1938), the fourth American to study under Wundt and the founder of the first laboratory under Catholic auspices, that of the Catholic University of America; the Benedictine priest Thomas Moore (1877–1969), a disciple and successor of Pace at Catholic University, who pioneered clinical psychology under Catholic auspices yet never formulated a defined Catholic context; William Bier, S.J. (b. 1911), a student of Moore's and the founder of the prodigal American Catholic Psychological Association; and the Franciscan priest James H. Vanderveldt, O.F.M. (b. 1893) and the layman Robert P. Odenwald, M.D. (b. 1899), both professors at Catholic University, who published *Psychiatry and Catholicism* (1952), a work that is admirable for its scientific scholarship and adherence to overt Catholic ethics but that nonetheless fails to achieve a penetrating integration. These early efforts and their lack of a highly integrated philosophical position would prove unequal to the task of withstanding the virulent ideology of scientism.

A *Catholic* Psychology?

Even when one critiques the attitudes of some of these Catholic pioneers who in *theory* gave primacy to the Catholic worldview, one is struck by a tenor of liberalism or secularism throughout. Edward Pace, the father of American Catholic psychology, was deemed "a dangerous liberal" by his

---

[5] The Würzburg school of psychology viewed judgments, thoughts, and meanings as determined by intangible mental activities as opposed to viewing cognition as a mere reaction to stimuli.

former fellow faculty member, Bishop Sebastian Messner. Along with two other liberal professors, Pace was recommended for removal from his teaching duties at the Catholic University of America by Leo XII's papal nuncio. The recommendation was never carried out, and the liberalism was passed down. Thomas Moore, Pace's successor at Catholic University and a rather uncritical proponent of Freudianism, was criticized for the questionable Catholicity of his psychology by his fellow faculty member, the illustrious churchman Fulton J. Sheen, and by a former student R. E. Brennan, O.P., who authored key works on Thomistic physiological psychology. William Bier, S.J., who also received criticism from Sheen for his attempts to make Freudian psychoanalysis palatable to Catholics, would at one time in his priestly career be reprimanded by his superiors for an excursion into ecumenism that was at the time forbidden, and would lead the American Catholic Psychological Association (see below) into dissent and finally apostasy.

At the least, it seems that these founders of American Catholic psychology, while still arguably within the pale of orthodoxy, were not sufficiently wary of the dangers of a psychology severed from the Catholic matrix. Maybe there was a lack of awareness of the moral and spiritual dangers inherent in a psychology free from Catholic anthropology. Perhaps the virulence of secularism was underestimated or the imperviousness of the faith was overestimated. In fact, the pre-WWI and pre-WWII worlds were safer, more *Catholic-conducive* climates than the transformed worlds that followed.

The deficiency of Catholic integration in the early stages of modern psychology is, on the one hand, surprising, since experimental psychology grew out of philosophical psychology, and a strong Thomistic presence in the Catholic development of psychology might therefore be expected. On the other hand, the fact that early experimental psychology was mainly concerned with the measurement of physiological phenomena (such as reaction times, reflexes, and sensations) would understandably impact the belief of some early Catholic psychologist that philosophy did not urgently impact *experimental* psychology.

However, while the nonrecognition of the consequences of experimental psychology severed from philosophy may be understandable, the nonrecognition of such severance in regard to *clinical* psychology is not. Indeed, the most serious consequences of not locating experimental psychology within a Catholic philosophical matrix would occur with the advent of clinical psychology. Clinical psychology, unlike experimental, seeks knowledge not for its own sake, but for the sake and good of the therapant. As such, it depends on the formulation of an anthropology, which is a philosophical and often theological construct.

In that clinical psychology springs from experimental psychology, the philosophical context of experimental psychology directly impacts the philosophical context in which clinical psychology is placed. Even the reductionist desire to keep experimental psychology completely quantitative/scientific by excluding any qualitative/philosophical context is itself qualitatively and philosophically contextual. By the time clinical psychology under Catholic auspices sprang from an experimental psychology (some fifty years after the Thomistic experimental psychologist Cardinal Mercier), the philosophical and Catholic content were, for the most part, excised, suspected, suppressed, or had waned. In any case, experimental psychology as practiced by Catholics failed to maintain within itself a strong philosophical heritage and, as such, was unable to bridge and transmit that heritage to the once-removed clinical psychology. As a consequence, clinical psychology was severed from its Thomistic foundations. Unlike the advent of experimental psychology, where Thomism and the possibility of a Catholic psychology was at least an issue, the once-removed clinical psychology rarely considered the issue. If it did, at best it merely sought to sanitize schools of personality (e.g., Freudianism) to fit the more overt moral strictures of the Church.

The closest clinical psychology came to being integrated into a Catholic worldview was in what may be termed the Catholic "characterological" genre. Before World War II, there were Catholic educational institutions that taught both experimental psychology and a rigorous Thomism. For the most part, psychology was not formally integrated with Thomism, but philosophy was recognized as a science of import equal to or greater than psychology itself. Individual psychologists and psychiatrists who grew up steeped in Catholic tradition and who were educated in Thomistic philosophy either in conjunction with or before their studies of psychology were involved in the emerging science of applied or clinical psychology. These Catholic clinicians integrated psychology into philosophy, if not systematically, at least in their own individual dispositions.

The characterological literature produced includes such classics as Reverend B. W. Maturin's *Self-Knowledge and Self-Discipline* (1915), Reverend Johann Lindworsky's *The Training of the Will* (1932), and James A. Magner's *Mental Health in a Mad World* (1953). This genre entails character development based on the Catholic philosophical understanding of virtue and vice and the theological understanding of nature and grace. Though it is based on a Catholic (Thomistic) worldview and promulgated by psychologists and psychiatrists, it does not systematically apply Thomistic principles to pathology or treatment. This characterological genre could also be called the genre of "commonsense," a commodity that was becoming scarce even in the early quarter of the twentieth century, when this genre found a receptive audience.

For the most part, these developers of the characterological genre adopted secular schools and located them into their own orthodoxy. As with the early Catholic experimentalists, such an integration was made possible by their own Catholic orthodoxy, learning, and zeal, not by a systematic integration. So while these men were clinical psychologists who were Catholic, they nonetheless did not develop schools of Catholic clinical psychology.

In a separate class of his own, because of his insight, impact, prominence, and prolificacy, is Rudolf Allers (1883–1963). Rudolf Allers was a member of the 1906 class of Vienna University medical school, the last class Freud taught as a faculty member there. Allers's formative mentor was Alfred Adler (1870–1937), a former colleague and subsequent critic of Freud who developed a school of psychotherapy or personality theory that became the leading rival of Freudianism, and one of the founders of personality theory. For a time Allers also worked alongside Emil Krapelin, the founder of modern psychology. Subsequent to his doctorate in medicine, Allers earned a doctorate in philosophy. It was Allers's philosophical astuteness that would cause him to break from the Adlerian school and become the leading critic of psychotherapy, especially Freudianism, which was taking the world by storm. Allers realized that the popular psychotherapies and personality theories brought with them a deficient, and, in his words, "heretical," philosophical anthropology. Allers's brilliant refutation of Freudianism and its claim to be scientific was published in *The Successful Error* (1940). Allers's critique of Freudianism was prophetic and scathing, and the myriad of works from other critics of Freud produced half a century later only built on his critique. In addition to his work on Freud, Allers wrote *Uber Schadelschusse* (1916), *Das Werden der sittlichen Person* (*The Psychology of Character,* 1930), *Sex Psychology in Education* (1937), *Self-Improvement* (1939), *Character Education in Adolescence* (1940), *The New Psychologies* (1940) and *Existentialism and Psychiatry* (1961). Upon immigration from Austria Allers taught for a decade at Catholic University as a professor of psychology in the School of Philosophy. He then transferred to Georgetown University as a professor of philosophy. Although Allers's critiques paved the way for a true Catholic integration of psychology, no one would take up the torch he left behind in the beginning of the tumultuous sixties.

Also of note was Conrad W. Baars, M.D. (1919–1981), a psychiatrist from the Netherlands, Baars, in collaboration with Anna Terruwe, M.D. (1911–2004), incorporated some Thomistic principles in his psychotherapy, while largely retaining secular psychodynamic models as his framework. Indeed, his most prominent work was based on the hypothesis that mental disorders stemmed from a lack of unconditional love experienced during the patient's early life, a major premise of humanistic psychology, especially that of Carl Rogers. However, Baars's approach far surpassed that of Rogers because of his sharing in the Catholic and Thomistic worldview and, specifically, his recognition that God was the source of all love.

Dissent and Heresy

In spite of these efforts, clinical psychology under Catholic auspices overall would only increase in heterodoxy and secularism after the great divide of World War II, so that the list of prominent Catholic psychologists of the latter part of the twentieth century would read as a list of liberals and dissidents. American Catholicism would contribute more than its share to this list.

Americans notable from among the list were John Cavanagh (1904–1982), a leading Catholic psychiatrist and Catholic University faculty member, who in 1968 joined nineteen other fellow faculty members in formally dissenting from Pope Paul VI's encyclical *Humanae Vitae*; Reverend Adrian Van Kaam (b. 1921), a disciple of Carl Rogers, once filled in for the anti-Catholic Abraham Maslow during a Brandeis sabbatical, and has since been busy inventing a nondenominational spirituality; Reverend William Meisneer (b. 1931) attempted to sacramentalize the psychoanalytic, or more aptly, psychoanalyze the sacramental, by equating spirituality with psychodynamics; Reverend Henri Nouwen (1932–1996), who was also involved in psychospirituality and was an immensely popular writer on that subject, was a champion of liberation theology and disseminated articles such as "Homosexuality: Prejudice or Mental Illness" (1969), which precipitated the American Psychological Association's and American Psychiatric Association's de-pathologizing of homosexuality; Sr. Annette Walters (1911–1978) was a close friend and disciple of the consummate materialist B. F. Skinner and an ever-waxing feminist whose extensive Church-funded education and doctorate in psychology did little to help her see the ontological impossibility of women priests.

This dissent culminated in the American Catholic Psychological Association's capping its heterodox career by formally dissenting from Paul VI's encyclical letter *Humanae Vitae* (1968) and audaciously questioning, from its vantage point of some thirty inconsistent years of clinical psychology, whether the Church in this teaching fully appreciated the nature of the person, conscience, and marital relationships.

Indeed, the trend of Catholic psychology in the twentieth century may be represented in the rise and fall of the American Catholic Psychological Association (ACPA). The ACPA was established in 1949 under the tutelage of William Bier, S.J. The ACPA dabbled in dissent from the beginning and, as mentioned, formally dissented in its criticism of *Humanae Vitae*. Bier, who had achieved some pre–Vatican II notoriety because of his illicit ecumenical activities, was the ACPA executive secretary until its demise in 1970. Bier was instrumental in both this demise and the organization's reappearance in 1971 as the non-Catholic, nondenominational Psychologists Interested in Religious Issues (PIRI). In 1975, when PIRI became affiliated with the American Psychological Association as Division 36, it gave up any pretense of being an organization whose members actually professed religious belief. In 1993 PIRI changed it name to Psychology of Religion, which best denotes its character as a secular entity that studies the phenomenon of religious belief—that is, it studies religion as a cultural and subjective experience—without validating that belief.

In Europe, the state of Catholic psychology was no better. Indeed, Cardinal Mercier's neo-Thomistic Louvain fell into the hands of Leo, later Cardinal, Suenens (1904–1996), who opened the university's doors to modernist academicians and whose advocacy, especially as a participant at Vatican II, of a psychology-based morality of personalism[6] paved the way for post–Vatican II dissent on the Church's teachings on human sexuality.[7] Beyond Suenens, a host of moral theologians have based their dissenting on psychology-based personalism. Some have been quite specific about psychology's influence. For instance, the influential, dissenting, and finally silenced moral theologian Bernard Häring (1912–1998) borrowed from Erik Erikson's theory of human development and came up with a new morality that defines sin as that which negatively impacts one's personal development.

In addition to the psychology-based personalistic moralities, a plethora of new age psychospiritualities have emerged in the wake of Vatican II. But the first psychospirituality to be dabbled in by Catholics was of the preconciliar era. Carl Jung (1875–1961) differed from Freud in his recognition of the spiritual and incorporation of it into his psychological conceptualization. Even such orthodox theologians as Bishop Sheen would approvingly quote Jung because he was religious, in contradistinction to the atheistic Freud. Jung was indeed religious but the religion he espoused was a neo-pagan one of his own creation and of which he was the prophet.

In the post–Vatican II era, Jungianism and other new psychospiritualities would flourish in the Church, especially within convents. A prime example of this is the Institute of Transpersonal Psychology in Palo Alto, California. Matthew Fox, the silenced heretical Dominican turned Episcopalian minister, whose sidekick was a self-proclaimed witch, is one of the guiding spirits of the Institute. The Institute's founder is Sr. Joyce Rupp (2000), a Servite nun who worships at the altar of the feminist god Sophia and esteems the works of Teilhard de Chardin (1881–1955) as prophetical.

Another example is the psychospirituality of the Enneagram, which has proliferated as a replacement of traditional schools of spiritual direction, especially as a replacement of the Jesuits' Ignatian Spiritual Exercises. Reverend Mitch Pacwa, S.J., a Jesuit who himself was seminary-trained in the Enneagram, points out its occult nature in *Catholics and the New Age* (1992). The noted moral theologian Monsignor William Smith (1993)

---

6 Personalism tends to weigh the subjective good of the person against the objective truth. In its most extreme form it holds that the good is what the person subjectively decides is good for him.

7 Cardinal Suenens, a strong proponent of feminism, was responsible for the personalistic wording in chapter 1 of part 2, the pastoral constitution *Gaudium et Spes* issued by Vatican II: "The Dignity of Marriage and the Family."

says of the Enneagram that "the more you read about it, the more it begins to resemble a college-educated horoscope; and that is not compatible with Catholic doctrine or practice. . . . As a tool for spiritual direction, it seems to me most deficient, even dangerous."

Before the post–Vatican II era, no churchmen could have imagined the diabolical influence that psychology would have upon practicing Catholics. However, Pope Pius XII (1876–1958), while being open to the science of psychology, was not unaware of its dangerous trends and issued stern warnings about its misdirection and misuse. In America, Bishop Fulton J. Sheen,[8] despite his naivety in regard to Jung, was one of the few pre–Vatican II voices from the Catholic intelligentsia to warn of the dire consequences that result from severing psychology from Catholicism. Pius XII and Bishop Sheen fought a losing battle. Psychology would become the Trojan Horse that would gain access to even the inner sanctums of the cloister, to therein disgorge a plague of a hedonistic neo-paganism.

Not until a decade or so after the post–Vatican II chaos, and a gaining of perspective and reaping of bitter fruits, were Catholic voices again raised in warning. The more prominent and prolific Catholic critic of status quo psychology is the psychologist Paul Vitz. Vitz has been a leading Catholic critic of both popular psychology and contemporary Western society. Among his many works is the influential *Psychology as Religion: The Cult of Self-Worship* (1977). In addition to Vitz, there have been other Catholic critics of modern psychology, including William Kirk Kilpatrick, who wrote the scathing *Psychological Seduction* (1983), and William Coulson, an erstwhile sidekick of humanist psychologist Carl Rogers who has repented of his misdeeds, especially his and Rogers's diabolical destruction of the Immaculate Heart of Mary order of nuns.[9] Thus, along with the works of Allers, there has been a substantial corpus of work that has powerfully and validly criticized and condemned modern psychology from a Catholic perspective.

---

[8] Sheen's dissertation, *God and Intelligence* (1938), was on Thomistic epistemology. He also penned semi-psychological works, such as *Peace of Soul*, based on Catholic spirituality and philosophy. He often highlighted Freudianism as a counter-Catholic ethos.

[9] See Appendix B, "The Psychovitiation of Catholicism."

The Catholic Psychological Genre

With the last decades' Catholic critiques of modern psychology and the regaining of Catholic sensibilities amidst the onslaught of secularism has come a growing awareness of the need to develop a psychological theory firmly ensconced in the Catholic worldview. Such a psychology is intrinsically dependent on a Catholic philosophy and theology, especially as it demarcates the teleological, epistemological, and moral nature of man. Though early pioneers such as Mercier, Maher, Thiéry, Peillaube, and Lindworsky, and those men of the characterological school (though in a less systematic way), tried early on to locate experimental and practical psychology within Thomism, strikingly little has been done in this direction in the latter half of the twentieth century. Indeed, the last hurrah seems to have been mid-century with the writings of two top-notch Thomistic philosophers and scientific psychologists. Robert E. Brennan, O.P., published an updated version of his classic *General Psychology: A Study of Man Based on St. Thomas Aquinas* (1952), and the prolific writer of textbooks Reverend Celestine N. Bittle, O.F.M. Cap., published *The Whole Man: Psychology* (1945). However, both Brennan and Bittle focused on experimental psychology rather than on psychotherapeutic theory.

The latter-century malaise that ensued despite these works may find a contributing factor in the newness of a metamorphosing clinical psychology, but it is the secularization of Catholicism that is the essential factor. This secularization caused the faith to be integrated into the matrix of secular psychology, rather than the science of psychology being integrated into the matrix of the faith. Whereas the proper dynamics would theoretically bring about the purification and correction of psychology by the influx of the Catholic worldview, that which actually occurred was a reverse dynamic that caused the Catholic worldview to become polluted and compromised. As a result, those who are staunchly orthodox and zealous in their Catholicity— that is, those who would have the motive to formulate an authentic Catholic clinical psychology—have tended to reject the "baby with the bath water," and thus scrupulously avoided a field that copiously spews the pollution of secularism. One very notable exception to this aversion is the recent work of Reverend C. Ripperger, FSSP. Ripperger's *Introduction to the Science of Mental Health* (2006) is a philosophical and theological analysis of the key areas in which psychology intersects with Thomism and Catholic teachings and practices. Though not intended to formulate a Catholic clinical conceptualization, this work promises to be an invaluable resource in the future development of such conceptualizations.

Vatican Pronouncements

And what of the Magisterium's view toward psychology? The statements of Pius XII and John Paul II, while encouraging and validating psychology and psychotherapy, are nonetheless rectifying prescriptions and warning proscriptions concerning the errors being promulgated by psychology. In 1953, Pius XII addressed the Fifth International Congress of Psychotherapy and Clinical Psychology. After accomplishing his *primary* purpose of delineating the errors present in modern psychology and providing rectifying principles, he concluded with: "Be assured that the Church follows your research and your medical practice with Her warm interest and Her best wishes. You labor on a terrain that is very difficult. But your activity is capable of achieving precious results for medicine, for the knowledge of the soul in general, for the religious dispositions of man and for their development." In 1958, shortly before his death, Pius XII again spoke on clinical psychology in his address to the Thirteenth Congress of the International Association of Applied Psychology:

> Psychology as a science can only make its demands prevail insofar as the echelon of values and higher norms to which We have referred and which includes right, justice equity, respect of human dignity, and well ordered charity for oneself and for others, is respected. . . . It is Our wholehearted wish that your work may ever increasingly penetrate into the complexities of the human personality, that it may help it remedy its weaknesses and meet more faithfully the sublime designs which God, its Creator and Redeemer, formulates for it and proposes to it as its ideal.

In a short address before the World Psychiatric Association and the American Psychiatric Association in 1993, Pope John Paul II stated that the "person is a unity of body and spirit, possessing an inviolable dignity as one made in the image of God and called to a transcendent destiny. . . . Indeed, 'freedom attains its full development only by accepting truth.' It follows that no genuine therapy or treatment for psychic disturbances can ever conflict with the moral obligation of a patient to pursue the truth and to grow in virtue."[10]

While accepting the validity of and need for clinical psychology, the Church has nonetheless warned of its harmful tendencies when removed from the adequate anthropology provided by the Catholic worldview. Unfortunately, these warnings have largely gone unheeded. Psychology under Catholic auspices has either diluted or sunk that Catholicity within the polluting pool of secularism.

Contra a Catholic Clinical Psychology

Despite the prophetic voices raised in both critique and warning, the overall fate of psychology under Catholic auspices in the twentieth century went from compromise to capitulation. This loss of Catholic identity was not just a haphazard slide, but rather a formal abandonment. The American Catholic Psychological Association's abdication of its unique Catholic identity and warp into the hyper-nonsectarian Psychology of Religion division of the APA both typifies and spearheads this trend in Catholic psychology. In the seminal and comprehensive work *Catholics in Psychology: A Historical Survey* (1954), Misiak and Staudt present the prevalent and subsequently prevailing argument of the time "that Catholic psychologists as a group do not meet [the] requisites of a distinct school and, hence, should not be considered a school of psychology" (280).

Misiak and Staudt present three arguments. The first argument states that because there is no philosophy that is inseparable from "Catholicism or Catholic scholarship or Catholic [philosophical] psychology" (279) there can be no distinctly Catholic school of clinical psychology. The major premise, upon which this statement is implicitly based, is true: that without at least an implicit philosophical framework there can be no distinct schools of clinical psychology.[11] However, their minor premise, that Catholicism holds no dogmatically accepted philosophical school, is faulty, and thereby renders invalid their conclusion that there is no distinct school of Catholic clinical psychology.

---

[10] John Paul II (1991, 1 May), Encyclical Letter: Centesimus Annus, 46.
[11] See in chapter 2, "Subalternating Psychology to Catholic Truth," and "Essentially Thomistic."

It is true that Catholics are not bound to accept any one philosophy, including that of Thomism, which is the philosophy that Misiak and Staudt specifically point out. While Thomism remains the perennial philosophy of the Church, there are other schools possible, such as those that emphasize the thought of the Church Fathers, Augustine, or Bonaventure. Indeed, Thomism itself admits of various schools: from a Thomism with classical Aristotelianism at its base to one that is wed to a modern phenomenology.

However, because of philosophy's status in the Church as the "hand-maid of theology," it is subordinate to the higher science of theology. This subordination requires that any authentic Catholic philosophy have in common certain essential philosophical conclusions. Theology, as it were, provides the essential philosophical conclusions. It is theology, not philosophy, that provides the specific difference of a Catholic philosophy and subsequently defines Catholic psychology.

It is Catholic theology that generates the unity of the various schools of philosophy by demarcating what schools are consistent with the teachings of the Church and thus qualify for being placed under the overarching general school of Catholic philosophy. Furthermore, much of the reasoning that leads to the essential philosophical conclusions required by Catholic teachings requires the acceptance of similar explanations, explanations that are often essentially Thomistic.[12] In any case, the theologically-generated unity of the various schools of Catholic philosophy is overwhelmingly greater than their diversity. They are therefore rightly deemed subcategories of a general school of Catholic philosophy. The presence of these related sub-schools of a general Catholic school of philosophy does nothing to diminish the integrity and validity of that general school.

The second argument that Misiak and Staudt advance is that

> even if all Catholic psychologists were adherents of the same Neo-scholastic philosophy, that fact would not make them one distinct school. First, there are Catholics in other branches of science, such as biology, chemistry, or physiology; and all of them accept Catholic theology . . . and most of them accept Neo-scholastic philosophy; and yet we do not speak of a Neo-Scholastic school in biology or in sociology or in physiology. (280)

---

[12] See in chapter 2, "Essentially Thomistic."

In short, Misiak and Staudt argue that since the other empirical sciences are not qualified by the Catholicity or philosophy of their practitioners, nor should clinical psychology be so. However, they fail to recognize that unlike psychology, the other empirical sciences do not deal with reason and volition, the elements that constitute the specific difference of the human person from other animals. Nor are other sciences concerned with the good of the whole person as is clinical psychology, and thus they do not require a holistic view of the person: a holistic view that is provided only by philosophical and, especially, religious understanding. Catholicism is more and more at odds with the devolving popular and secular understanding of the person. As such, a Catholic psychology will be increasingly unique in its conceptualization of both the person and what it views as the good of that person: a good that includes mental health.

Finally, Misiak and Staudt point out that a distinct school of clinical psychology "does not merely connote philosophical premises but implies the use of specific methods and emphases on certain topics or fields which are peculiar to this school" (280) and that Catholic clinical psychology does not meet this criterion. The following chapters' espousal of a Catholic clinical psychology's foundational principles and introduction of Imago Dei Psychotherapy will, it is hoped, convincingly belie this assertion.

CHAPTER **2**

● ● ●

Foundations of a Catholic Clinical Psychology

IMAGO DEI Psychotherapy (IDP) is based on a Thomistic conceptualization of mental health. The validity of any Catholic qua Catholic clinical psychology is determined by how fully it adheres to and applies the Church's theological and philosophical understanding of anthropology, especially in regard to teleological, epistemological, and moral considerations. Imago Dei Psychotherapy's Thomistic base best assures adherence to the Church's understanding of the person, since Thomism is the *philosophia perennis*, singularly proved, validated, and recommended by nearly a millennium of ecclesiastical scrutiny and usage.

Imago Dei Psychotherapy is also existential in its orientation. IDP's specific existential orientation is derived from the Thomistic seminal emphasis on *esse*, or "being." This existential orientation is well suited to a science that is both clinical and humanistic.[1] In addition, the existential orientation of IDP gives primacy to the person's transcendental yearnings, viewing man as "a seeker of truth." Finally, existentialism, with its kinship to phenomenological perception, is well suited to the needs of the clinician, who must be aware not only of the empirical manifestations of pathology, but also of the therapant's subjective experience of reality. In the context of Thomism, this existential/phenomenological orientation allows the clinician to enter into the subjective experience of the therapant

---

[1] IDP does not ascribe to a Thomistic phenomenology but rather to a paleo-Thomism that is existential in its *esse* orientation and the employment of a clinical observation that is phenomenological. See Chapter 10.

without discarding objectivity, thus allowing the appraisal and rectification of that subjectivity when it is discordant with objective reality.

As the name signifies, Imago Dei Psychotherapy is ordered to *restoring the image of God* in man when that image is marred by mental illness and/or characterological distortion. The *imago Dei* is precisely man's rational/volitional nature. The restoration of the therapant as the image of God is directed by the principle of Thomistic moral agency, where the fully human act entails rational assent to truth and a subsequent volitional embracing of this truth as the good. This moral agency conceptualization finds its expression in IDP's *Moral Agency Schema* which is the blueprint to Imago Dei Psychotherapy's therapeutic interventions.[2]

Though Imago Dei Psychotherapy at present apparently stands alone as a therapeutic systemization of Catholic clinical psychology, it is nonetheless proper that it be viewed as a sub-school of Catholic clinical psychology. The therapeutic definitiveness required of a formal school of psychotherapy entails certain emphases (and thus certain exclusions) that, if held, as benchmarks would unnecessarily preclude future valid applications of the principles of Catholic clinical psychology.

Indeed, the principles herein presented as foundational not only to IDP but to any authentic Catholic psychotherapy are themselves subject to categorization, emphasis, and expression in various combinations. Even so, regardless of the arrangement of these principles, they remain in essence the same, for they are derived from the Catholic Church's essential theological and philosophical anthropology, or understanding of the human person. This anthropology entails both epistemological, moral, and teleological principles. As such, the validation of any particular Catholic qua Catholic clinical psychology will be determined by how fully it adheres to and applies the Church's understanding of the human person in regard to his nature, his reason for being and destiny, his way of knowing, and his good.

The Catholic Advantage

"If we could descend on our subject from above like Catholic theologians, with our fixed definitions of man and man's perfection and our positive dogmas about God, we should have an easy time of it" (James 1882, Lecture

---

2 See chapter 8.

XIV). Unfortunately William James, a nebulous dabbler in Christianity at best, could not so descend, for lack of the elevation of faith. Even so, he was inadvertently prophetic, for so to access the truths of elevating faith produces an unparalleled advantage in discerning the nature of man and the subsequent remedying of that nature. As such, Imago Dei Psychotherapy boldly accesses, indeed submits to, the full corpus of Catholic teachings that it might best assure the efficacy of its psychotherapeutic interventions.

For two thousand years, the Church has dispensed the deposit of faith[3] that was entrusted to her, by expounding theologically and philosophically upon the truth therein. As such, the matchless advantage a Catholic clinical psychology has over non-Catholic ones is the anthropological insights granted by and garnered from divine revelation and guaranteed by the Holy Spirit. Catholicism weds to divine revelation a corpus of philosophical truth that exceeds any other philosophy in its depth, breadth, harmony, and systematic exposition. This unique ability of Catholicism to wed itself to philosophy is due to Catholicism's being uniquely true, for only a completely true religion welcomes the complete scrutiny of reason.

Within a Catholic clinical psychology the question is not whether divine revelation exists or whether faith enlightens reason, or even whether the Catholic Church is the God-ordained guardian of revelation and the infallible teacher of the truths of the faith. These are questions that must be answered in the affirmative before one enters into the practice of a Catholic psychology, or any other Catholic qua Catholic endeavor. Merely entertaining theoretically the proposition that faith can inform and clarify reason will not produce the synergism of the actual process; one needs actually to have the faith.

> It is not possible to say: Let us assume that the Christians are right and let us see where this assumption carries us. For one can only "see" it, that is, one catches sight of the light that falls from the truth of religion upon reality, only if one identifies oneself existentially with what is believed. . . . Most discussions on this subject are sham discussions. In reality they deal with an entirely different subject, namely, whether theology is possible at

---

3 "That body of revelation, containing truths to be believed and principles of conduct, which was given by Christ to the Apostles, to be preserved by them and their successors, with the guarantee of infallibility" (Attwater 1961, 143).

all, whether anything like revelation exists and, if so, how do we recognize it, what grounds there are for faith—and so on. (Pieper 1991, 147)

This does not mean that a nominally Catholic or non-Catholic clinician cannot follow or respect a certain formula in his dealings with Catholic therapants, but that such a following of formula will be necessarily superficial and unable to respond spontaneously and with faith-filled insight to the unique exigencies of the Catholic therapant, and thus will lack the full Catholic advantage. The inadequacy is made more apparent when the therapant himself, which is often the case, ascribes to a formulation of faith that either is not being lived with integrity, is deficient, or is somehow heterodox.[4] But regardless of the therapant's religious orientation, be he a believer or an atheist, a clinician's efficacy will gain its full potential only when the clinician himself existentially identifies with the fullness of the Christian faith that is Catholicism and integrally subalternates his clinical practice to that faith.

Any Catholic, no less a Catholic qua Catholic clinical psychologist, must base his worldview on the belief that the Catholic faith is absolutely true.[5] Catholicism, unlike any other religion, is absolute and definitive, claiming with a divine boldness that her teachings are infallible and enunciating and cataloging these teachings in the most definitive way so as to subject them to the scrutiny of reason. Her concise, unambiguous philosophical and theological formulations, scrupulously recorded in logical expostulation and detailed in her own dogmatic history, would leave her in a precarious position indeed if not for the divine guarantee that is hers.

---

[4] The need for an integral faith and Catholic worldview is present for all Catholics. The presence of "disconnects" is often highlighted in psychotherapy and is the root of many "splits" in personality. Once a therapant becomes cognitively aware of these disconnects or dissonances, he is poised to remedy them by supra-therapeutic practices, such as prayer, penance, the sacramental life, and religious study, all of which will increasingly conform his thoughts and behaviors to his Catholic ideals, and hence to Christ.

[5] The brilliant Anglican convert John Henry Cardinal Newman (1906) wrote: "It is, then, perfectly true, that the Church does not allow her children to entertain any doubt of her teaching; and that, first of all, simply for this reason, because they are Catholics only when they have faith, and faith is incompatible with doubt. No one can be a Catholic without a simple faith, that what the Church declares in God's name, is God's word, and therefore true. A man must believe the Church is the oracle of God; he must be as certain of her mission, as he is of the mission of the Apostles" (Discourse XI, 215).

Her absolute claim to be the one true Church of Christ, infallible in matters of faith and morals and authoritative in their teaching, means that what the Church proclaims definitively is without exception the truth. If but one instance can be found where she is or was wrong, her entire edifice would fall; if even one of her formally taught truths can be shown to be false, or contradictory to the other myriad of truths she holds, then the whole edifice crumbles. This assurance is the tenor of the Catholic mindset, and when one gains it through faith and reason it procures for him the vantage point of the faith: a perspective that allows greater critical and insightful discernment. As a Catholic seeks truth, it is the faith that allows him to see its limitless expanse. Some faith can blind one to truth, but the Catholic faith is completely rational.

The corpus of Catholic truth is like a magnificent tapestry that has been woven over the ages. Each truth, each thread, is crucial to the integrity of the multicolored and intricate design, and each thread upon the closest of inspection can be found to be in its place. The existence of such a monumental, unmatched tapestry of truth testifies to the divine nature of its Weaver and the indefectible nature of His ecclesial loom, the Church.

Essentially Thomistic

Accessing divine revelation and Catholic theology is of essential import for the general understanding of human teleology, man's end or reason for being, while the need to access the philosophical becomes progressively more apparent as the study moves from the area of teleology to the areas of epistemology and morality. While epistemology and morality are more within the realm of philosophy than of theology, these subjects, most especially when they are Thomistic, nonetheless flow from, are perfected and validated by, the theological.

No other philosophy has been so theologically validated as has Thomism: "Thomas Aquinas is not speaking of philosophy as it can be found in the mind of an unbeliever. Himself a theologian . . . , Thomas speaks of the philosophizing reason of baptized men" (Gilson 1960, 30). It is St. Thomas Aquinas's logic, empiricism, systemized investigation, concise expostulation, and, most importantly, assent to and immersion in God's truth via supernatural faith and adherence to Catholic teachings that provides the philosophical formulation by which all others are measured.

Because Thomism is intrinsically informed by sacred doctrine, it has a lofty perspective that allows it to see and evaluate the entire field of philosophy and avoid being blinded by its own philosophical conceptualization. Thomism's preeminence, then, is specifically because of its unique supra-philosophical nature. Thomism's *supra-philosophical nature* entails openness to and use of divergent philosophies, past and future, Christian or not, that express truth. This in itself is because of Thomism's—or more fundamentally Catholicism's—radical openness to all truths as a manifestation of absolute Truth, be those truths empirical, philosophical, or divinely revealed. Gilson (1960), comparing Thomism to other philosophies that share a similar inner coherence, wrote:

> The doctrine of Thomas Aquinas has this superiority over the others: that its principles are, in a sense, the same as those of apparently different, and sometimes opposed, philosophies—with this difference only: that in Thomism these principles are taken in the fullness of their meaning. . . . *All that is true in any other philosophy can be justified by the principles of Thomas Aquinas, and there is no other philosophy that it is possible to profess without having to ignore, or to reject, some conclusions that are true in the light of these principles.* Speaking in a more familiar way, one can be a Thomist without losing the truth of any other philosophy, whereas one cannot ascribe to any other philosophy without losing some of the truth available to the disciple of Thomas Aquinas. (278)

Some "philosophies" are open to all and sundry truths because they lack any internal coherence or are undefined and ambiguous, and therefore are pseudo-philosophies or pseudo-sciences. Other philosophies have an internal coherence similar to Thomism, but the very fact of that coherence shuts them off from truths outside their philosophical system. Thomism, and Thomism alone, by the very fact of its internal consistency and unity, is open to all truths and able to incorporate them into its philosophical system.

The preeminent status of Thomism is secured by the unmatched advantage it garnered from Aquinas's own brilliant intellect, his deep accessing of sacred doctrine and use of the unmatched illumination it affords, and his sanctity and mysticism that illuminated sacred doctrine itself.

> To see the general structure of Thomism is, at the same time, to realize the twofold nature of its vocation. It is a philosophy inasmuch as every-

thing in it hangs on the truth of a first metaphysical principle. On the other hand, what offers itself as the supreme results of a purely philosophical reflection on the principles can just as easily be interpreted as the conclusion of a meditation on the meaning of . . . the truth gratuitously revealed by God to man in view of man's salvation. (280)

Thomism has as its two certain endpoints empirical experience and revealed truth. By means of logic, it produces a philosophy that connects these two certain points (Figure 2.1). Though the line of reasoning that runs to and fro from the points of empirical truth and revealed truth may admit of some breadth that allows variation, it is a breadth limited by the relentless dictates of logic. John Paul II (1992), who in the strict sense was not a Thomist, stated that "the Church has been justified in consistently proposing St. Thomas as a master of thought and a model of the right way to do theology" (43) and that "the realism of Thomas could recognize the objectivity of truth and produce not merely a philosophy of 'what seems to be' but a philosophy of 'what is' " (44). Benedict XVI (again not a strict Thomist but more Augustinian) said that St. Thomas Aquinas "with his charism as a philosopher and theologian, . . . offered an effective model of harmony between reason and faith."[6]

Figure 2.1.
Philosophical Line of Reasoning
Connecting the Two Points of Certitude.

Empirical Truth's   Revealed Truth's
Point of Certitude   Point of Certitude

Thus Thomism is a philosophical line of reasoning that is certainly correct in its orientation, and it produces at least the essential components of a truly Catholic philosophy and, as such, the foundations of that which would be deemed a truly Catholic clinical psychology.

Because Thomism embraces both the empirical and the theological, it provides the ideal nexus between psychology and revealed theology. The Thomistic conceptualization of a hierarchy of sciences that views the empirical science of psychology as subalternated to philosophical science and philosophy as subordinate to (the "handmaid of") theological science makes uniquely possible a true integration of the three realms of knowledge.

---

6 Angelus address, Vatican City, January 28, 2007.

The choice of Thomism as the philosophy on which to base a Catholic psychology is clear-cut. Although there may be other possible philosophical schools that could render an authentic Catholic clinical psychology,[7] none is more suited for the job than Thomism. Leo XIII (1879, ¶18) stated, "[R]eason, borne on the wings of Thomas to its human height, can scarcely rise higher, while faith could scarcely expect more or stronger aids from reason than those she has already obtained through Thomas." The consistent and singular magisterial approbation of Thomism guarantees that it renders a metaphysics that is harmonious with Catholicism and thus preeminently suited to provide the context of a Catholic clinical psychology.

Reality Based

It will be advanced that within the Thomistic and Catholic understanding of the person, and as implemented in Imago Dei Psychotherapy,[8] the specific concern of clinical psychology is the ability of the person *to perceive, receive, reflect upon, and act upon the real.* The ability to perceive is a function of physiology and sensation. The ability to receive reality is what Aquinas terms abstraction, and it, along with the ability to reflect upon reality, are functions of reason. The fourth criterion, the ability to act upon the real, is the function of the will or volition.

Unlike secular psychology, whose purpose is defined broadly, and even nebulously, as seeking to promote "health and human welfare" in "all aspects of the human experience,"[9] IDP espouses a definitive specification of clinical psychology's end. However, this specification diminishes neither the scope nor the importance of clinical psychology, but on the contrary, mandates that scope and emphasizes that importance. The processing of the real (receiving and reflecting upon it) and the subsequent acting upon

---

[7] It is because of Thomism's supra-philosophical nature that Catholicism can espouse Thomism without being only Thomistic.

[8] Though the author believes that this definition of clinical psychology's end as the ability of the person to perceive, receive, reflect upon, and act upon the real is of the essence not only of any Catholic psychological conceptualization, but of psychology in general, its very definitiveness recommends that at present it be considered a principle of a specific application of Catholic theoretical principles, viz., that of Imago Dei Psychotherapy.

[9] American Psychological Association (2002), Bylaws I.1, and www.apa.org/about/, respectively.

the real involves all of man's faculties and every facet of his existence; and this processing and acting are the very human difference, that which makes man a rational free moral agent.

The general Thomistic principles of epistemology and morality are based on the foundational and unifying Thomistic metaphysical principle of *esse*, or being. Aquinas defined the real, the true, and the good as being. Thomistic ontology holds that being, reality, truth, and the good are the same entity viewed from different operative points of view. To understand the controvertibility of being, reality, truth, and the good is to ground existence firmly in an objective order, allow appraisal of one's subjective ability to grasp and act in accord with that order, and integrate all aspects of experience from divine revelation to mundane calculation.

The Thomistic concept of being is based upon an understanding of God as the only essential being, as the ultimate truth, reality, and good. Inherent in this Thomistic understanding is the position that the human person's final end, the very reason for human existence, is to know truth and possess it as the good by being united with Supreme Being. *Being, reality, truth, and good* refer to the same entity and its analogies because God is the Ultimate Being and Reality, the Truth, and the Absolute Good.[10]

For purposes of therapeutic intervention,[11] Imago Dei Psychotherapy distinguishes these different aspects of being as follows: when being is encountered as *being-as-such* (which is the apprehension that things exist without yet abstracting how they exist in their specificity), it is encountered existentially or experientially, that is, precognitively, and is herein termed *reality*;[12] when being is the object of the intellect it is *truth*, for "truth is the proclamation of being" (Hilary, quoted in Pieper 1989, 112); and when being is the object of the will it is termed the *good*, that which is desirable.

When a man acknowledges "He who is, the pure unlimited act of being" (Gilson 1960, 279)—he acknowledges his own creaturely relationship with God as well. This realization is the essential truth about one's existence, and

---

10 See in chapter 5, "Analogy of Being."

11 See in chapter 8, "The Thomistic Moral Act."

12 In IDP the term "reality" is used both commonly and as the specific precognitive or existential experience of being-as-such. Because of this specific technical use of the term "reality," the term "the real" is used in IDP's formal definitions to refer to all aspects of being.

thus forms the basis of self-identity and self-knowledge, which are the bedrocks of therapeutic intervention.[13]

Subalternating Psychology to Catholic Truth

While a Catholic clinical psychology will admit of some diverse theological and philosophical emphases, just as the Church admits of some diversity, it must in essence remain harmonious with a Catholic anthropology and teleology. Just as there are some variations of what may be deemed an authentic Catholic philosophy, so too there are some potential variations of what may be deemed an authentic Catholic clinical psychology.[14]

Much of the differences in future schools of Catholic psychology will be based on the different metaphysical and theological nuances that are found in the respective schools of philosophy on which they draw. Subtle differences may exist, for instance, between one psychologist's understanding and another's understanding of volition and habit, just as it does with Catholic philosophers and theologians; nonetheless, free will must always be upheld as an essential human element and key to the Catholic anthropological understanding of the person.[15] Though a Catholic clinical psychology may manifest these theoretical nuances in a concrete form, giving rise to some variation in Catholic schools of psychology, in essence it will be united, and even the accidentals will be more similar than not. So too each school, if it is truly based in orthodox Catholicism, will adhere to some form of conceptual realism (the ability truly to know reality) and

---

[13] True psychological insight is both objective and holistic, but the field of psychotherapy is fraught with erroneous understandings of insight. For example, humanistic psychology defines insight as finding out what is most pleasing to oneself, and thus bases insight on subjective feelings and self-interest. Freudian insight is reduced to understanding one's psychosexuality, which is a relatively mundane element of one's existence. In Freudianism, this error is compounded by an erroneous understanding of psychosexuality itself.

[14] As of yet, with the exception of this treatise's introductory presentation of Imago Dei Psychotherapy, such sub-schools do not formally exist because Catholic clinical psychology is still in its nascent form

[15] For instance, the Jesuits and the Dominicans have traditions of philosophy and spirituality that nuance the role of volition and grace differently, yet when the practitioners of these traditions remain orthodox they are substantially united in the essentials of their definition.

profess belief in revealed truth, which are the two endpoints upon which the perennial philosophy of the Church, Thomism, is based. The principle that allows this underlying unity of Catholic clinical psychology is that of *subalternation*.

Pius XII stated, "There are those who have thought it necessary to accentuate the opposition between the metaphysical [i.e., the philosophical] and the psychological. A completely wrong approach! The psychic itself belongs to the domain of the ontological and metaphysical" (1953, ¶12). In its formulation, a Catholic clinical psychology unites the empirically scientific and the philosophic, with empirical science being contained under, or subalternate to, philosophy. Furthermore, philosophy itself is guided by sacred theology. The Catholic understanding of integrating the qualitative with the quantitative, of locating psychology within the Catholic worldview, is specifically defined as a subalternated relationship, whereas the secular argument for clinical psychology's general need of qualitative worldviews or philosophies is nebulous and open-ended. This is because secular psychology's understanding of what is meant by "the good of the whole person" is itself nebulous, whereas the Catholic argument for such a need is definitive and absolute.

From a Catholic perspective, psychology is a lower science necessarily subalternate to or contained under the higher science of philosophy.[16] Philosophy is a higher science because it studies the mind and man in a more complete and abstract manner than does psychology; that is, it is able to study the spiritual essence of the mind, whereas psychology cannot. The requirement to view the mind as essentially spiritual is due to the Catholic faith principle that man is essentially spiritual. Man's intellective powers— that which makes man reasonable—must be spiritual because man is still essentially man and a unique reasonable being even when his soul separates from his dead body. Thus, the empirical method of psychology is not able to engage its formal object, the essentially nonmaterial mind, but rather must depend on philosophy to engage the spiritual object of the mind and

---

16　The term *science* entails not merely empirical science but "any organized body of knowledge of things through their causes." When science is thus defined then philosophy is a science superior to the empirical, because "it studies the essences and nature of causality as such, which is completely beyond the scope of the empirical" (Ripperger 2000, 5).

define it. In short, psychology must accept the findings of philosophy as facts. Using St. Thomas Aquinas's example, just as music depends on the facts of arithmetic for its composition and performance, but cannot in itself determine the principles of calculation,[17] so the science of psychology depends on factual findings of philosophy for its working content, but cannot in itself determine the principles of the nonempirical.

Thus Psychology Is Subalternated to Philosophy

The subalternation of psychological science to philosophy, and specifically to philosophical or rational psychology, is fundamental to any psychology that claims to be Catholic. In contradistinction to materialism, the most elementary characteristic of Catholicism is its acknowledgement and reasoned elucidation of the nonmaterial, or spiritual, realm. In contradistinction to psychological scientism, where man, and specifically the mind, is viewed as purely physical, Catholic anthropology holds a highly defined hylomorphism where man's essence, that is, his rationality and volition, is found in the nonmaterial soul. But whereas scientism does not accept the nonempirical, Catholicism does accept the empirical.[18] A Catholic clinical psychology, then, does not reject any authentic empirical or experimental aspects of psychology, but because of the immateriality of the soul, it cannot be only, or even predominately, an empirical or experimental science. It is proper to define a Catholic clinical psychology as one in which the science of psychology is integrally subalternated to philosophical psychology, which in turn is guided by sacred theology. However, this subalternation admits of a reciprocal dynamics: just as philosophy, being the handmaid of theology, facilitates authentic theological formulation by the validation of reason, so does empirical science facilitate authentic philosophical formulation by the validation of observation and induction.

In sum, an authentic Catholic clinical psychology views itself as necessarily subalternated to Catholic philosophy because Catholicism definitively holds that the mind is an essentially spiritual entity of the soul. It is philosophy that studies the non- or meta-physical, not empirical science. Thus, clinical psychology is incompetent to study its own final end.

---

[17] *De Trinitate*, q.5. a.1., p. 3 (Ripperger 2000, 3).
[18] For a brief outline of the Catholic roots of the empirical sciences, see Appendix B.

Ripperger (2000) specifically delineates the subalternation of psychology to philosophy as follows:

> Psychology is subalternated first and foremost to the philosophy of man since it receives its understanding about man's nature and the nature of man's faculties from this science. . . . [It] is also subalternated to metaphysics, for it is proper to metaphysics to discuss what is not in matter nor in motion. Since the intellect, will and other faculties in man are spiritual, at least *in radice* if not entirely, then only metaphysics can adequately discuss their nature. . . . Psychology is subalternated to logic insofar as logic is the art of right reasoning and in order for the intellect to be healthy, it will have to comply with the principles of logic. Psychology will be subalternated to epistemology since that science tells us the nature of man's knowledge, his intellect and how he knows. It will be subalternated to ethics insofar as ethics treats of the appetites and their right ordering and how they affect morally right and wrong behavior. (9–11)

All of these philosophical sciences are guided, informed, and enlightened by sacred theology: God's revealed truths entrusted to His Church. Sacred theology requires that certain essential philosophical principles be in harmony with its revealed truths. An example of an essential philosophical principle would be hylomorphism (man's soul-body composition), a truth that is both of divine revelation and of natural reason. Such a correspondence on a multitude of principles allows philosophies to be validated as "Catholic" or not, and in varying degrees. Although this process does not lend itself to producing one singular Catholic philosophy in all its specificity, it does recognize degrees of congruity between philosophies and sacred theology. It is by such a process that Thomism is seen as the most congruent and, as such, most highly validated of philosophies.

Finally, a Catholic clinical psychology recognizes the grave necessity of subalternating its science to its philosophy and submitting its philosophy to sacred theology because of its subject matter. A botany severed from a Catholic philosophy will have few ill effects because of its nonhuman and thus amoral subject matter. Even the medical sciences, though here the issues become more critical, can for the most part get by with a bare philosophical content such as the pre-Christian Hippocratic oath (though application of the oath often requires more subtle reasoning). But psychology is the most sensitive of sciences, its subject matter the most human, for it deals with that which makes man *man*: his rationality and volition.

The doctor of psychology studies and intervenes in the most delicate realm of the mind. Here at the locus of the human incarnation, at the conjunction of the rational soul and neurological organicity, a twilight pervades in which the borders of the spiritual and the physical become indiscernible. Thus the ramifications are great; indeed, they are eternal, for the doctor of psychology touches the very essence of man. Nowhere outside of the spiritual realm is a person more vulnerable than when as a therapant he bares his very soul in order to heal his mind.

What foolhardiness then not to recognize the absolute necessity of a Catholic clinical psychology! There can be no separation of faith and reason, of philosophy and science, when the subject matter is the rational soul and its concomitant organicity. Tragically, this is exactly the abdication that has occurred among the mainstream ranks of Catholic psychologists.

CHAPTER **3**

● ● ●

IDP's Teleological and Anthropological Bases

T**HE JUSTIFICATION** and urgency of the advent of a Catholic clinical psychology is found in the following hypothesis: *the science of clinical psychology will attain its full efficacy only when located within a Catholic anthropology.* In his 1953 address to the Fifth International Congress of Psychotherapy and Clinical Psychology, Pope Pius XII enunciated minimum requirements for the general secular field of clinical psychology. He stated that an adequate consideration of the person requires that he be considered as a total psychic unit, a structured unit, a social unit, and a transcendent unit. That is, an adequate consideration of the person must employ a basic Catholic anthropology, regardless of the clinician's or therapant's religious orientation, for human nature is human nature regardless of a person's belief system.

Pius XII recognized that the science of clinical psychology is unable by itself to reach its final end, and thus must be located within qualitative (philosophic or religious) worldviews. Clinical psychology as an empirical science can fathom only the materially measurable; however, its end is the good of the whole person, and the person's essence is spiritual. It is only the qualitative sciences that can study the nonmaterial. Specifically, psychology must be subalternated to philosophy because the Church teaches that man's essence is the nonmaterial soul which determines and governs him as a psychosomatic unit, and only philosophy can study the immaterial.

Clinical psychology is unique among the sciences. Clinical psychology differs from academic and theoretical sciences because its method of scientific inquiry and resultant findings are not ends in themselves; rather, clinical psychology is not ultimately or even immediately concerned with knowledge for its own sake, but with the good of its human subject.

Because clinical psychology is concerned with the integral good of the entire person, it also differs from the other clinical and humanistic disciplines that are ordered toward benefiting an aspect of the person. Medicine, for instance, is similar to clinical psychology as a clinical discipline, yet differs in being formally concerned with a person's physical health rather than with his whole person. In relation to the social sciences, such as economics or politics, clinical psychology again is unique because of its study of the whole person and its goal of achieving the overall good of that person. In relation to the humanities, clinical psychology differs in its utilization of scientific method to study and clinically intervene on behalf of the whole person. Literature, for example, is concerned with studying the whole person, but it does not employ scientific method nor is it clinically applied.

Clinical psychology, then, can be specified as a discipline that utilizes the scientific methodology of the quantitative and empirical, that is, of the measurable and observable, yet must draw on the qualitative and metaphysical,[1] that is, the philosophical, to achieve its humanistic end. *Being both scientific in its means and methods and humanistic in its end, clinical psychology qua psychology is in the predicament of not being able to achieve its own final end by relying only on its specific scientific means. It is only the scientific method, and not qualitative interpretation, that is within psychology's specific realm of competence.*

In order to encompass the person in his nonquantifiable dimension and achieve its final end of the good of the whole person, clinical psychology must avail itself of that which is outside its realm of scientific competency. Clinical psychology must access a qualitative, metaphysical worldview that is able to enunciate the anthropology or nature of the person. Such a worldview may be explicit or implicit; it may be elaborately theistic, as exemplified in the great world religions; or it may be radically reductionistic, where the person is indeed viewed as comprising only that which is scientifically measurable. Yet, again, it is not within the competency of the

---

[1] Even those psychologists who formally hold a reductionist view of the person or hold that the only authentic knowledge is the quantifiable (which is itself a *qualitative* judgment) must, it seems, acknowledge that they and the profession do not have the authority or grounds to exclude that which admits of the nonquantifiable or qualitative, such as philosophical, literary, or religious truths.

profession of psychology to determine definitively this qualitative medium, this worldview.[2]

Faith and Reason

The philosophical or qualitative requirements for a secular psychology become more explicit and defined when applied to a Catholic psychology. A Catholic psychology requires the formulation of anthropological principles derived from essential teleological, epistemological, and moral truths of the faith.

In some formulation or another, any authentic Catholic clinical psychology must equate mental health with a correspondence to reality, since Catholicism is based on the understanding that reality is an objective phenomenon that emanates from God and is discernable by man.[3] Imago Dei Psychotherapy's specific definition of mental health is *the ability to perceive, receive, reflect upon, and act upon the real.* Such a reality-based definition of mental health makes even more apparent the need for the science of psychology to access qualitative categories. Understanding the nature of man's encounter with reality goes beyond mere scientific issues of physiology and neurology and depends on the answer to questions such as *whether or not man can know reality,* and, as such, *what is the nature of man and reality.* As will be seen, the answers to these questions ultimately depend on the answer to the questions of *whether God exists* and *what his nature is.* Such ultimate questions only philosophy and theology can answer.

> To philosophize means . . . to concentrate our gaze upon the totality of encountered phenomenon and methodically to investigate the coherency of them all and the ultimate meaning of the whole; to examine what "something real" actually is, what man himself is, mind, the complete total of things. (Pieper 1991, 147)

Theology goes beyond philosophy and spans both faith and reason, for theologizing is "endeavoring to discover what really was said in the divine revelation" (148).

---

[2] For a review of secular literature on the relationship between psychology, philosophy, religion, and Catholicism, see Appendix C.

[3] That God Himself is Reality or Being and that man can discern this reality is explicated in subsequent chapters.

A Catholic clinical psychology, then, will depend upon the insights of philosophical reasoning to inform scientific reasoning and upon the light of faith to clarify and guide philosophical reasoning. It is this synergy of faith—*the* faith—and reason that is the specific difference of a Catholic clinical psychology.

A religion's worldview understanding of the relationship of faith and reason determines the dynamics of integrating that faith's contents with reason's philosophical and empirical findings. The Catholic worldview holds that "faith supports reason and perfection; and reason, illuminated by faith, finds strength to raise itself to the knowledge of God." So proclaimed Benedict XVI in his Angelus address[4] on the feast of St. Thomas Aquinas, and so has been the Catholic understanding of revealed truth and rational truth for two thousand years. From the beginning there has been no compartmentalizing of truth in Catholicism: faith illuminated reason, both philosophical and empirical, and reason scrutinized and systematized faith. The wedding of the Catholic faith to classical Western philosophy not only preserved the best of ancient Greek thought but rectified and perfected it in the penetrating light of revelation, thus producing schools of philosophy that can truly be said to be the fruits of the faith.

Reason's components of philosophic knowledge (which is qualitative and deductive), and empiric knowledge (which is quantitative and inductive) work together to inform and validate each other, so too these components of reason work synergistically with faith. The Catholic understanding of the dynamics of faith and reason is reciprocal. A Catholic integration entails not only faith informing and enlightening reason but also reason validating and expressing faith. That is, a valid faith should be harmonious with reason if all truth, revealed or natural, is held to emanate from the mind of God. This does not mean that all truths of faith are fathomable via reason alone, but that those truths of faith that are fathomable via reason do not contradict that reason.

Revealed truth can also illuminate reason in its own discoveries. Much as flashes of intuition aid the process of deduction by providing insights that serve as points of reference, thus allowing the philosopher (or poet) to triangulate on these points like a navigator and locate certain truths, so does revelation provide him with the reference points within which all

---

[4] Vatican City, January 28, 2007.

truth is located. Revelation, like intuition, often provides the answer so that one can work backward and construct the solution's formula. Most importantly, unlike intuition, revelation as taught by the sacred Magisterium of the Church is infallible, providing absolutely certain reference points of truth.

In accord with man's essential existential orientation, both reason and faith ultimately have the same end: to discern the purpose of human existence, which is the glorification of God. Faith perfects reason. Faith sheds light upon obscure truths that are barely accessible to reason and facilitates their understanding. The horizon of faith is required to bring the findings of reason together into an integral whole, to synthesize and integrate knowledge toward its singular goal, its final cause and end. Thus faith enables relational knowledge and gives rhyme to the reason. Without faith, reason is informational at best, and remains fragmented and compartmentalized. In the context of faith, reason also acknowledges its limitations.

A fragmented, unsynthesized knowledge is akin to an information overload, where the onslaught of information can lead to an unprocessed cacophony. Schizophrenia has been described as just such a phenomenon. So too, when a person does not recognize the limits of his intellectual capacities, he utilizes a criterion of a grandiose or egotistical personality. This is the case when one denies that there can be any truth that is not measurable or discoverable by his own unaided reason. Faith, then, fosters mental health by its integration of knowledge and its demarcation of the intellect's limits.

Complete openness to truth is the hallmark of the Catholic worldview. It is the infallible truths of faith and morals as enunciated by the Magisterium and both qualitative and quantitative truths of reason that make up the whole truth. Hence the entire gamut of truth—from the most mundanely empirical to the most sublimely speculative—is essential to a Catholic clinical psychology that aims at facilitating a therapant's openness-to-reality.[5]

---

[5] Although truths of faith need not be overtly presented to a therapant, they nonetheless are essential for the clinical insights of the therapist. However, recognition of the existence of God and the universal moral norms of natural law, both of which are foundational to this acceptance of truth, are not of faith but of reason (see chapter 10). Openness-to-reality is the fundamental prerequisite for mental health (see chapters 6 and 8).

The Teleology of Secularism

Secular psychology's teleological premise can never suffice for a Catholic psychology. Any presence of this premise can only harm the integrity of a Catholic psychology. The secular premise holds that a person's ability to adapt or function in his milieu and his "feeling good" is the sum of man's teleology. The criteria listed in the American Psychiatric Association's *Diagnostic and Statistical Manual of Mental Disorders*, Fourth Edition Revised (*DSM-IV-TR* or *DSM*), are essentially concerned with a person's ability to *function socially and economically with the absence of distress or painful symptoms.*

Functionality is the most measurable and urgent proximate end of clinical psychology, and dysfunctionality, to a large extent, is the way clinical psychology defines mental illness. The *DSM* maintains that mental disorders are associated with a significant increased risk of distress or disability and the present loss of freedom. Disability is specified as "impairment in one or more important areas of functioning" (American Psychiatric Association 2000, xxxi). The advent of the empirically supported protocols further promotes functionality as the main criterion for mental health.[6]

While functionality may be the most urgent and tangible objective of clinical psychology, it should not be the only objective. Indeed, to limit intervention to the restoration of functionality is to limit intervention to the treating of *symptoms*, not *causes*. Whereas the pursuit of personal happiness or human fulfillment may find a foundation in functionality, this pursuit's specific goals may transcend mere functionality in as many ways as there are individual philosophies of life, indeed individuals. And, again, if the discipline of psychology is defined as "embracing all aspects of human experience," then experience that is not merely "functional" must be admitted. This elevation of functionality by the American Psychological Association may be seen as manifesting a post-Catholic West's materialistic, industrial/technological ethos.

---

[6] Empirically supported (validated) protocols are an attempt by the profession to standardize treatment. The exigencies of managed care have mandated their establishment; however, that which is measured is necessarily of a symptomatic nature. Therefore, empirically supported measurements are ordered toward the immediate effects of treatment (i.e., functionality and how one feels) and are insensitive to indicators of deep psychotherapeutic change, which goes beyond the treatment of symptoms and treats the cause of the symptoms.

None of this is to imply that functionality should or can be replaced as the touchstone by which mental health is judged. However, it does warn against the tendency to exclude worldviews that have values other than the utilitarian, pragmatic, and materialistic ones of functionality. Indeed, the profession of psychology's anthropo-teleological premise of functionalism and feeling good is radically deficient and even antithetical to a Catholic anthropo-teleological view, where *the good of man is a question not of function or feeling, but rather of assent to the truth*. This assent is the act of the will par excellence; and it may or may not be milieu adaptive and functional or conducive to feeling good at all; indeed, at its height it entails prophetically contradicting the wisdom of the world and embracing suffering.

IDP's Teleological Basis

A Catholic clinical psychology will have a unique emphasis and manner in which it applies techniques and therapies. It will also give rise to unique interventions (e.g., one that facilitates a therapant's intellectual assent to the existence of a Creator). A Catholic clinical psychology will also bar certain techniques and interventions because of moral or anthropological reasons. However, the specific difference of an authentic Catholic clinical psychology is not to be found in the means per se but in the ends to which those means are ordered. It is the end goal or teleology of the person that makes a Catholic clinical psychology unique. Only the Catholic Church enunciates theological truth (and thus man's teleological truth), with an absolute certainty and with a full sufficiency. Also, as mentioned previously, it is sacred doctrine that is the final adjudicator of truth in both the philosophical and empirical realms.

Revealed truth makes known not only God but also His creation, especially man, who is created in His image. As such, the Church, who is the sole guardian and teacher of divine revelation, has an unrivaled insight into human existence. The Catholic Church's understanding of the universe as a manifestation of divine reason proved the key to discovering the ordered teleology of that universe; so too, and most importantly for clinical psychology, it is the Church's understanding of human existence that holds the key to man's teleology or true end. This certain teleology together with the epistemology and morality that branches from it comprises the anthropological foundation upon which a Catholic clinical psychology is built.

The Catholic understanding of the purpose of human existence can be summarized in the following revealed truths: (1) man is created in the image of God, and his final end is union with God; (2) original and actual sin mars this image and bars man from his final end; (3) God became man to undo the damnation of sin by the propitiation of His sacrifice and proffering of forgiveness and grace; (4) man can once again achieve sanctification and salvation, and superabundantly, if he contritely accepts Christ's forgiveness and responds to His grace. It is from this revealed teleology of redemption, sanctification, and salvation that the essential philosophical truths concerning man are validated and clarified.

It is the Catholic Church that is commissioned to apply revealed truth and infallibly guide the faithful in their journey to God. The Church exists solely to usher men out of sin and foster their sanctification, salvation, and eternal union with God, and thus glorify God. A Catholic psychology is properly ordered toward facilitating (though not necessarily presenting) this ultimate teleology of sanctification and salvation, and does so in a precursory effort that aids therapants in their recognition, acceptance, and embracing of reality, that is, of truth and good.

The Teleology of Sanctification

It is primarily from the truths of faith that the reason for man's existence and his final end is derived.[7] As per the *Baltimore Catechism*'s beautifully concise summation of the Church teaching on human teleology, man was created "to know, love, and serve the Lord in this world, and be happy with Him forever in the next."

The Church's teaching on human teleology can be stated more tersely still: *to be a saint.* "Be perfect, as your heavenly Father is perfect" (Mt 5:48). This process of sanctification is very simple; one must merely give his *fiat*, say "yes," to God's will for him. But though the process of sanctification is simple, it is not easy, for it takes an all-consuming effort. For the zealous Catholic bent on union with God all else is secondary, indeed expendable,

---

[7] Philosophy—a function of reason—can render only an incomplete teleology. A completely philosophical teleology will in essence produce either a here-and-now eudaemonistic orientation (be it a refined and lofty Aristotelianism or a coarse and degenerate hedonism) or it will produce a fatalistic orientation (be it a disciplined stoicism or an anarchical nihilism).

in pursuit of this one goal. Neither riches, nor health, nor reputation, nor even family is substitutable for sanctity; and surely none of these goods is a sign of sanctity. Indeed, it is the very vows of poverty, chastity, and obedience that are the characteristics of those who are specially chosen. Suffice it to say that the pursuit of sanctity is an all-pervasive goal that colors and orders all facets of human life. In Catholicism, unlike classical Protestantism, grace builds upon nature, and nature is transformed by grace.

The impact of Catholic teleology on a clinical psychology located within the Catholic worldview is immense. No longer is functionality the end-all of human existence, but rather sanctity, which may, indeed will, confound the calculations of functionality. The Catholic philosopher Josef Pieper (1989) wrote:

> It insults the dignity of man's spirit to lead a life so much confined and imprisoned within narrow considerations of immediate usefulness that his own small environment utterly ceases to be a window on the larger "world." To be thus totally absorbed in a mere fragment of reality, to "function" rather than live, is not human. . . . For life to be truly human it seems indispensable that every so often the domain of practical work and effectiveness be shaken up and brought down to size by the challenge, disturbing yet fruitful, coming from the world's ultimate reality. (96)

It is the Church's duty so to shake men up. In her counsels of perfection—poverty, chastity, and obedience—she witnesses respectively against the world's insatiable greed; against its consuming lust and hedonism; against its pride and Luciferian *non serviam*. When the Church's followers give themselves wholeheartedly to her and her Bridegroom, they share in her incarnate prophecy and become the martyrs and saints whose very existence confounds the world.

To live out one's life successfully, according to the Catholic worldview, is to achieve sanctity and to gain heaven. All else—indeed one's very life—derives it worth from this teleology of sanctification and salvation.[8] A

---

8 "From a Catholic perspective, a life story is essentially a story of a soul. All that finally matters for the zealous Catholic is the conformity of his soul to Christ, his personal sanctification. Therese of Lisieux, like all saints, realized and acted upon this truth with complete integrity and commitment. . . . In the eyes of the world, and certainly today's world, many facets of her life would be deemed imprudent and even fanatical. A bourgeois France viewed a fifteen-year-old girl's rush into an

Catholic worldview then does not hold functionality by itself as the indication of the health of the soul or mind. One may be extremely functional but pathological (as many of the great successes of the world have been, driven as they were by their personal demons), or one may be dysfunctional according to the norms of the world (as is One who is ignominiously put to death on a cross at thirty-three) but sane (as sane as Truth itself).

Catholic teleology is both proximate and final. The transcendent final end is happiness with God, the beatific vision. Although this transcendent teleology is ordered to a happiness not of this world, it does manifest itself in this world and is essentially connected with earthly existence's proximate ends. These proximate ends, the teleology of the *here and now* where one is "to know, love, and serve the Lord," prescribe duties that surely bring joy but also entail suffering and self-abnegation. The redemption or sanctification of suffering—that is, suffering's positive aspects—is a crucial element of a Catholic teleology and sets a Catholic clinical psychology glaringly at odds with that of the secular, which simply seeks (as *DSM-IV* states) to alleviate "present distress" or "a painful symptom" and restore functionality. Suffering is essential to human motivation, growth, and fulfillment, and it is the sine qua non of sanctification.

Hence, human teleology, as infallibly enunciated by the Church, is derived from both a proper understanding of epistemology and morality. However, when presented clinically, revealed Catholic teleology need not be explicit, nor should it be "preached" to the therapant. It can be reduced to a nonrevelatory level not by posing the *answer* of faith but rather by making the therapant aware of his intrinsic questioning nature. Thus, man's call to truth and beatitude is made manifest in his *questioning* nature. IDP aims primarily to help the therapant come to realize that his teleology is to *seek the truth*, while the disposition of the answer is a sec-

---

austere cloistered convent—and her father's facilitation of it—as odd behavior. (Suburban America would consider it nothing less than bizarre.) Acquaintances of the Martin family said that the rigors of Carmel, the fasts and the cold, would be too much for the young Therese. And their warnings were correct; she was to die nine years later of an illness especially associated with the lack of nutrition and warmth. Surely there were at first indictments of 'I told you so.' But it soon came to light that Therese Martin had died a saint, and the bourgeois tongues stopped wagging; and today even suburban Catholic America—with its standard of spiritual compromise—has taken St. Therese of Lisieux to heart" (Dilsaver 2001, 29).

ondary consideration.[9] So while the nature or even the existence of truth may not be discovered in the therapeutic process, the essential quest, in all its urgency, should be.

Catholic teleology is made manifest in the therapant's discovery of a philosophical questioning and spiritual search that is innate to his nature as a human being. In doing so, the therapant also begins to feel a call to something infinitely greater than himself, and begins to sense the greatness and sublimity of his human vocation. The source of man's anxiety is in his often suppressed or disguised sense of his contingency. Therapy is ultimately aimed at bringing the therapant to the brink of existential truth, where he recognizes his particular being within the context of *being* in general (and where he is in the position to exercise authentic faith). This ability to reflect upon one's existence and truth is what makes man an intellectual substance and spiritual being in the image of God.

IDP's Anthropological Basis

From a Catholic teleology based on revealed truths—and thus one that infallibly delineates man's *raison d'être*—springs a sound epistemology, a right morality, and an adequate anthropology. Again, Catholic teleology is concisely prescribed in the classic catechetical question and answer: *Why did God make you? To know, love, and serve Him in this world, and be happy with Him forever in the next.* This formulation also entails the essential epistemological, moral, and anthropological truths about man. *Knowing God* entails the knowableness of truth (epistemology), the ability both to accurately perceive it and to reflect upon it. *Loving God* requires that man be able to choose freely that which is true and good (morality). *Serving God* mandates that man act in accord with that which he chooses. One must first know God before he can love Him, and one must first love God if his actions are to be in His service.[10] Finally, man's destiny of union with God defines him as a being (anthropology) who is capable in sharing in the divinity of God.

---

[9] While IDP does not in essence include evangelization, catechesis, and spiritual direction—all of which are the competency of the Church—this does not bar these from being incorporated into the therapy when appropriate.

[10] "The act of the will cannot be said to be good, if an evil intention is the cause of the willing" (Aquinas, *ST* I–II, q. 19, a. 7).

A Catholic anthropology is derived both from reason and from revelation. Reason yields the universal observation that man differs from other beings by means of his ability to think abstractly and make free choices. This is his specific difference, that which makes him *Homo sapiens* (the wise). If the good is that to which man is ordered, and if man is specifically a rational being, then his good is specifically a rational one. Rationality, however, is not to be limited to a strict reasoning process. It includes volitional processes or, in poetic terms, processes of the heart. As Blaise Pascal (1623–1662) wrote, "The heart has reasons that the mind knows not" (154*n*423).

Revelation further defines this philosophical, empirical classification of man as a rational, volitional being. The fundamental anthropological truth of revelation is that man is *imago Dei*, made in God's very image: *Let us make man to our own image and likeness* (Gen 1:26). "This image of God is not found even in the rational creatures except in the mind" (*Summa theologiae* [hereafter *ST*] I, q. 93, a. 4); or as Gilson (1960, sec. 28) put it, "Man represents the kind of being God is, because like God he too is an intelligent being" (36).[11] As extrapolated upon in the discussion on epistemology,[12] man's immortality is due to the spiritual nature of his rationality. So too, it is his rationality, which has the ability to become that which it knows, that gives man the potential to become divinized by knowing God.

In the Imago Dei conceptualization, clinical psychology is ordered to the restoration of the mind's rational image. When the mind is restored it is capable of achieving its end, that which it was made for, which is truth. Since all sensate life seeks its particular good, and since man's specific difference is his rationality, his specific good is of the rational order, that is, man's specific good is the truth. Truth is that which conveys reality, and IDP views mental health as the ability to perceive, reflect upon, and act upon the real. Hence, epistemology, which is the process of knowing, and the nature of truth itself are of the utmost importance for any clinical psychology.

The incarnation of Our Lord Jesus Christ gives the truth of man being created in God's image a deeper meaning. It gives man a divine and perfect

---

[11] "Now all beings resemble God in that they are; some of them resemble God in that they live, and finally, some resemble God in that they know by means of intellect and reason. These bear to God the closest resemblance of all, so they are said to bear His image in their very being and to that extent they belong, so to speak, in a species similar to that of divinity" (Gilson 1960, 36).

[12] See chapter 4, "The Spiritual Nature of Intelligence and Knowing."

prototype for being that image of God. The Incarnation also allows man to embrace fully the mystery of suffering, which is concentrated in the passion and death of Christ. Finally, the ability of man to become divine, because of the Divine becoming man, means all men are redeemable. The ultimate fact of the Incarnation guides and informs Imago Dei Psychotherapy and the clinician who practices it, even if this dynamic is invisible to the therapant.

Hylomorphism: Soul Plus Brain Equals Mind

Where is it that the brain leaves off and the soul begins, where the neuro-physiological gives way to the spiritual? Is psychology the study of the soul, the brain, or the intellect? Literally, psychology is the "study of the soul." In a Catholic clinical psychology such as Imago Dei Psychotherapy, this literal meaning remains, for the soul is the essence of the person and the animating principle of the body; its immortal welfare is also the *raison d'être* of Catholicism. Still, a Catholic psychology's concern is not so much with the condition of the soul (a priestly competency) but rather with the powers of the soul and how they are manifested in the organicity of the person. Specifically, a Catholic psychology is concerned with the conjuncture of rational soul and brain, the synergistic sum total of which can be deemed *mind* or *intellect.*

So while psychology is not simply the study of *gray matter*, it is certainly the study of a *gray area.* For the question will always remain: where does the physical organ leave off and the spiritual begin? In practice, this may be a moot point, for the spiritual powers of the soul require intact organicity for their full actualization; that is, the powers of the soul require the means of the brain to express themselves and thus be discernable. An extreme example of this is found in the *autistic savant syndrome*, where, because of organic brain damage, otherwise severely mentally impaired individuals display the rarest of genius in one or two areas; for instance, instantaneous complex mathematical calculation or perfect musical performance recall. In this phenomenon it appears that the powers of the soul—themselves undiminished but frustrated by the organic malfunction—are concentrated into one intact organic avenue of actualization.[13]

---

[13] Traditionally and poetically in the West, the heart has been thought of as the seat of the soul (in the East it is the abdomen) because it is here that the sympathetic

For a psychology to be Catholic, it is absolutely necessary to allow for a nonmaterial dynamic that informs the biological basis of psychology. "Man is composed of an organic body and a rational, spiritual, and immortal soul, which coalesce into one nature" (Tanquerey 1959, 399). It is the soul that makes man man: "Whoever presumes to assert, to maintain, or to hold that the rational or intellective soul is not the form of the body per se and essentially, must be regarded as a heretic."[14] That is, and in accord with a Thomistic philosophy, spiritual "powers of the soul" must inform the organism of the brain. Without such spiritual powers, mental activity becomes purely physical and physiological. If this is held to be the case, then mind equals brain; but in that it is the mind that makes us who we are, both generally as rational beings and specifically as a unique person, it would follow necessarily that man is in essence a material being, which is a heretical proposition. Not only are the erroneous psychological/anthropological theories based on the materialistic view of man heretical, but the many psychotherapies based on this view must be barred from a Catholic clinical psychology's armamentarium, and readmitted only if and when they can be sanitized and augmented.

S. Pinker's reasoning is representative of the mind equals brain position:

> The doctrine of the ghost in the machine is that people are inhabited by
> an immaterial soul that is the locus of free will and choice and which

---

nervous system is felt in correspondence to cognitions and emotions. Scientifically, but still poetically, if there is one area that can be said to "house" the soul it is the brain. Even though the soul cannot literally be encompassed by matter, it is the life and organicity of the brain that specifically makes possible mortal human life, for man's specific difference from the other animals is his rationality. Some argue that once the brain is dead human life is impossible and the soul has departed. Again, that lack of the requisite neurological organicity, for example, in the case of an encephalitic infant, human life qua human is impossible; that is, human ensoulment is not present because there is no possibility of the soul expressing its rationality. Others argue that human ensoulment does take place because the potentiality lies in the embryonic genetic make-up and embryonic teleology of the infant, regardless of the physical defect. Philosophically, it seems that the latter position is the correct one since partial diminishment of neurological function does not diminish the humanity of the impaired, nor does the absence of a physical possibility impact spiritual potential. Ethically, that is, when deciding whether or not a neurologically deficient person has the right to life, acceptance of the latter principle is mandatory.

[14] This an infallible *(de fide)* statement of the Church as proclaimed by the Council of Vienna (1311–1312).

can't be reduced to a function of the brain. . . . But neuroscience is showing that all aspects of mental life—every emotion, every thought pattern, every memory—can be tied to the physiological activity or structure of the brain. (Cited in Callahan 2002)

This assertion that there is a neurological basis of all thought, feeling, and emotion—that is, the physiology of the brain as the source and essence of personhood—is based on the fallacy of equating correlation with causation.

> It is quite possible that, from any mental activity, neuroscientists can abstract a mechanical aspect and associate it with certain thoughts, emotions, and so on. But that in no way "reduces" the mental activity to a "function of the brain." All that it demonstrates is that thinking, too, has a mechanical aspect to it. To move from that fact to the notion that those mechanical processes "cause" our thoughts is akin to deciding that, because we can abstract out certain aspects of any city and call that abstraction a "street map," that therefore street maps are the cause of cities! (Callahan 2002)

St. Thomas Aquinas's philosophical explanation of man's essentially spiritual mind is found in his teachings on the powers or faculties of the soul. Indeed, Aquinas does demarcate where the organicity of the brain leaves off and the spiritual intellective powers begin. Aquinas held that there is a cogitative intellect that grasps sense images. It is in this *cogitative* intellect that Aquinas locates the last limits of the organic or the physical. Aquinas held that there is an *agent intellect* that abstracts the universal and therefore immaterial concept from the object sensed. It is in this agent intellect that are found the beginnings of the spiritual, or nonorganic.

Man has two types of knowledge: that of the particular, which is manifested in individual material beings, and that of the universal, which by definition is never manifested in a particular material being. If the object of the cogitative intellect is the particularity of the material, then the cogitative intellect too must be material. The Thomist C. Ripperger (2000, 66) locates the cogitative intellect in the frontal lobes. The next step in knowing is the nonmaterial abstraction of the universal. This step requires an intellective faculty that is itself nonmaterial. This nonmaterial or spiritual faculty is what Aquinas terms the agent intellect. So, though the agent intellect depends on the organicity of the cogitative intellect in order to abstract the universal and immaterial idea from the material and particular image, abstract thought itself does not take place in an organic structure such as the frontal lobe. Again, correlation is not causation.

While the particulars of St. Thomas Aquinas's epistemological mechanics or explanation are sound and useful for the development of any clinical psychology, his conclusions—which his epistemological explanations preeminently support—are absolutely essential for a Catholic clinical psychology. These conclusions are that man can truly know reality or truth and that this process of knowing takes place within the spiritual cognitive faculties. It must be posited that man can know truth; otherwise neither revelation, which is the knowing of supernatural truths, nor Christian teleology, which is the knowing of God that culminates in the beatific vision, is possible. It must be posited that man's essence, that is, the specific difference of his rationality, is a spiritual intellectual soul that is substantive; that is, man's soul is immortal and able to exist on its own beyond the death of the body. As will be seen in the next chapter, the very ability to know requires a spiritual intellective faculty.

A Fallen Race

Man's intellective and volitional faculties both are debilitated; for though man was created in God's image, this image has been distorted, his nature wounded, because of original sin. The first effect of original sin is the *loss of sanctifying grace*, where man's holiness was lost and he was placed under the tyranny of the devil. The second effect is the *loss of preternatural gifts*, which are wounds to man's nature. These genetic wounds are comprehensive,[15] wounding the intellect, the will, and the body. In the corporal realm, man's body is subject to suffering and death. In the psychological realm, man's intellect is darkened because of the wound of *ignorance.* Thus he easily falls into error because he has difficulty recognizing what is true, especially practical and moral truth, and is inclined to consider temporal things rather than eternal things. Man's volition is weakened because of the wound of *illwill.* Thus he has difficulty overcoming vices and cultivating virtue. Man's passions are disordered because of the wound of *concupiscence.* Thus the pas-

---

[15] "The entire Adam was changed in body and soul *for the worse.*" *Decrees of the Council of Trent,* Session V, canon 1.

sions, or sensual appetites, do not heed and are insubordinate to the dictates of reason. Because of these psychological wounds to the intellect and the will, man is in general prone to evil. Original sin and its effects, which remain even after its remission,[16] distort man as the image of God.

The astounding anthropological truth of man being made in God's image and the tragedy of that image's distortion is surpassed only by the anthropological truth of God becoming Man and the tragic triumph of His sacrificial death. The Incarnation, which offers the remedy for man's impaired relationship with God and a balm for the ensuing wounds, provides the final answer to "Who is man?" by making him more than he was, for now God and man share a common nature.

Modern psychology is to be justly credited for categorizing and even discovering many of the mental ills that plague mankind. However, there has been a tendency to think that psychology also has discovered the anthropology of the person. This is a drastic mistake. To think so reduces man to the quantifiable, to the dissectible, to the predictable. Man is *imago Dei*, made in the very image of God; therefore he is an abiding mystery.

To presume that modern scientific psychology qua science has finally discovered the correct anthropology is audaciously to discount the wisdom of the ages as well as revelation: a wisdom and revelation that is synthesized in the Catholic Church's anthropology of the person. The core truths of Greco-Roman philosophy and Judaic theology provide the pillars of a Catholic anthropology and Truth Himself, the Incarnate God, provides the foundation.

---

[16] See in chapter 10, "Sin, Evil, and the Demonic."

CHAPTER **4**

● ● ●

IDP's Epistemological and Moral Bases

THE CHURCH'S philosophical understanding of epistemology and morality, like her anthropology, is intrinsically linked to dogmatic Catholic teleology. Catholic teleology holds that man is intended to assent to truth, and this assent is meant to culminate in the ecstasy of an ever-expanding beatific vision of the Truth. Therefore, anthropologically, man must be *one who seeks the truth*, and epistemologically he must be *one who can know the truth*. Truth is the ultimate good, and the will is that which acquires the good by means of the moral act.

Homo sapiens is the "wise," he who knows that he knows. As such, man is concerned with whether his perceptions are true or not: he is concerned with the truth. All sensate life seeks its particular good, and since man's specific difference is his rationality, his specific good is of the rational order; that is, his specific good is truth. In that truth is the manifestation of reality, and mental health is the ability to perceive, receive, reflect upon, and act upon the real; the process of knowing and the nature of truth itself are of the utmost importance for any clinical psychology.

This chapter will touch on a few core Thomistic concepts of epistemology, or the process of knowledge acquisition, that are crucial to a Catholic clinical psychology. It is recognized that within the greater context of Catholic philosophy, and to some extent within Thomism itself, there are differing schools. As such, what are herein advanced as epistemological touchstones are those Thomistic principles that IDP considers indispensable for any authentic Catholic worldview and philosophy and that are, at the same time, particularly germane to the practice of clinical psychology.

Prevalent epistemological positions that are not compatible with the Catholic worldview will also be examined. The nature of truth itself will be enunciated in accord with a Thomistic and Catholic worldview. Finally, since the object of the truth becomes the object of the good when it passes from cognitive consideration to volitional desire, free will and the acquisition of the good in the moral act will also be discussed.

A Philosophical Epistemology

Empirical science properly studies the mechanics of physiological sensorium, that is, sensate perception and neurological processing. Yet an adequate epistemological theory depends on more than the merely physiological; it depends on the philosophical. "What is reality?", "What is the nature of truth?", and "Can man grasp reality and truth?" are primary philosophical questions that are aspects of the supreme philosophical question, "What is being?" Catholic philosophy equates truth with being. Merely uncovering the physiological mechanics of perception and reflection will not answer whether or not there is an integrity of the perceptual and reflective processes, that is, whether or not what one perceives and reflects upon is true. As such, the scientific, quantifiable mechanics of the physiological processes of perception and reflection, even if known perfectly, would not render an adequate epistemology. In addition, an adequate Catholic epistemology requires a philosophical framework because of the nature of the intellective process itself. In that Catholicism holds that the soul is that which makes man reasonable, *intelligence is at essence a spiritual phenomenon* that is understandable only through metaphysical reasoning.

The Spiritual Nature of Intelligence and Knowing

As the soul is spiritual, so is knowledge. Philosophically, the nonmateriality of knowledge can be seen in the nature of concepts. Most concepts are of a universal nature: *man* and *tree* can refer to a general type of being. Yet all material being is particular: it is either *this* man or *that* tree. While particularity, the sine qua non of materiality, may be found in particular words, words are not concepts themselves but only represent concepts (as is evidenced in the presence of different languages); nor are universal concepts merely the result of seeing that certain beings have something in common.

One immediately abstracts (see below) the essence of a thing even before he can catalogue it. That is, one can truly know a being on first acquaintance, when the being encountered is as such a *sui generis* being (a unique being); otherwise there would be no being known a priori with which to compare subsequent beings. "One triangle is sufficient to form the concept of a triangle" (Sheen 1938, 108). Since a part cannot be greater than its whole, a concept, which is universal, cannot be of the particular, material order.

It is the theological necessity that finally assures that knowledge, and the intellective process, is spiritual. The intellective process must be essentially spiritual, since both the angels and God are incorporeal intelligent beings. "Thou hast made him a little less than the angels" (Ps 8:6; Heb 2:7). Whereas the angels *are* intellects, because of their purely spiritual substance, man can be said only to *possess* an intellect; for man is not simply a spiritual substance, but a corporal one as well. So too, man is made in God's image: "Let us make man to our own image and likeness" (Gen 1:26). Man is the only animal created in the image of God, and God is spirit. Man's specific difference among animals is his intellect. It necessarily follows that man's intellect is spiritual.

Man's intellectual resemblance to God is also that which allows him to know God. If the intellect were material it could not know God, who is spirit. It is by means of the spiritual intellect that man becomes like God by knowing Him, a knowing that finds culmination in the beatific vision.

The psychological task of restoring the image of God in man is thus primarily an intellectual or cognitive process. Since intellectual clarity, the ability to reflect upon the truth, is impacted by volition (the ability to attend to higher truths and goods at the expense of lower truths and goods), psychotherapy must also include behavioral aspects. Moreover, because man is also a physical being who through sensation acquires knowledge, his physiological condition is also of concern. Nonetheless, the essential dynamics of a Catholic clinical psychology remains an intellective one: facilitating the therapant's assent to Truth.

Conceptual Realism

St. Thomas Aquinas's recognition of both revealed and empirical truths and of both the spiritual essence and the material means of the intellective process resulted in his highly defined and comprehensive epistemological theory known as *conceptual realism*. Centuries before the advent of modern empirical science, Catholic philosophical psychology may be said to have gained in the apogee of Thomistic conceptual realism an irreplaceable and unsurpassable insight into the general dynamics of the epistemological process. Although the Thomistic explanation of the processes of knowing may not be as nuanced or intricate as the process really is (a possibility that Aquinas himself surely expected),[1] the Thomistic explanation nonetheless provides the essential steps and corresponding types of faculties that are required for the true acquisition of knowledge.

It is philosophical epistemology, not the scientific, that is generally of most concern to a psychotherapeutic clinical psychology.[2] The inability to translate sense perception into a coherent understanding of reality can stem from either physiological or psychological factors. The inability to accurately perceive sensation is not a psychopathology, but rather a physiopathology. For example, the physiological diminishment of vision does not diminish one's sanity; however the intellectual and volitional inability to assent to truth does.

As such, it can be expected that the application of the specific explanatory dynamics of Thomistic conceptual realism to clinical work will yield an increase in the efficacy of therapeutic technique.[3] Yet, even the mere Thomistic conclusions concerning the spiritual nature of knowledge and

---

[1] Aquinas wrote, "Our cognitive power is so imperfect that not even the nature of one single gnat can ever be entirely understood" *(Expositio super symbolum Apostolicum)*.

[2] The physiological manners of perceiving and processing reality are primarily the concerns of experimental psychology, neuropsychology, and physiology.

[3] The specific explanatory dynamics of conceptual realism can be studied in such works as Ripperger's introduction to the science of mental health: *Philosophical Psychology*, Vol. 1(2000) or Sheen's *God and Intelligence*, which are cited in the bibliography. A brief outline follows: In the tradition of Aristotle, Aquinas divides the intellect according to specific powers or faculties. The first is a material entity called the potential intellect, which receives sense experience from the world. The potential intellect includes common sense faculty, memory, imagination, and the cogitative faculty. The second is a spiritual entity called the actual intellect, which has the power to abstract the form from beings encountered through sense experience. The third, also spiritual, is called the acquired intellect, which is the power to reflect on the facts and upon its own operations. In addition, both the actual and acquired intellects require a causal power to actualize their potential; this is called the agent intellect.

knowing are enough to give conceptual realism an immeasurable superiority over the materialistic epistemologies that are prevalent in clinical psychology. The minimal epistemological conclusions of Thomistic conceptual realism (or any variation thereof that is harmonious with the Church's anthropology and theology)[4] that are absolutely necessary for a Catholic clinical psychology are those conclusions that are also necessitated by revelation. These conclusions can be condensed thus: *Truth is knowable because the intellective process is spiritual.*

Truth Is Knowable

It has been demonstrated both philosophically and theologically that the intellect is in essence spiritual. This spiritual intellective process makes possible the second essential postulate: in his knowing, man abstracts the truth, the reality, or the essence of a thing. "Only a philosophy that upholds a spiritual faculty can explain even the possibility of knowledge" (Sheen 1938, 139). If a divine concept or idea (the Scholastics call this the *form* of a thing) is not at the essence of being, of a thing that exists, then that being is incomprehensible; it has, as it were, no rhyme or reason, and concepts are merely unreliable creations of the mind. One cannot know a being that is not the result of a creative concept because there is nothing to know; one can only experience or react to the sensation of such a being. The belief in an intelligent Creator, however, locates the essence of all being in a concept of the Creator. There is rhyme and reason to all beings. Man's ability to know this essence, or nonmaterial form of a thing, is made possible by the nonmaterial nature of his own intellect.

Conceptual realism is commonsensical. It is taken for granted that one can indeed discern reality and can validly reflect on this reality, which is

---

[4] Even an epistemology as closely resembling Thomism as the Scottish Protestant minister Thomas Reid's (1710–1796) realism is crucially deficient. For Reid the truth of common sense finds its impetus from a "common subjectivism," the common consent and the common perception of the masses. Whereas in a Thomistic realism the impetus is derived from the thing perceived; it holds the truth within its being, and the mind is so designed as to recognize that truth. The weakness of Reidian realism is again the tenuousness and uncommonality of common sense, especially in an age of mass propagandization. Reid was forced into this modified realism by his adherence to Protestantism, for as an authentic conceptual realist he would have been faced with the mandate of a non-subjective ecclesial teaching authority, of an objective Christianity, viz., Catholicism.

the premise for everyday activity. Man can intentionally and effectively interact with his environment because he can discern reality and truth. Conceptual realism holds that this ability is made possible by the process of abstraction. That which is abstracted is the essence of the thing perceived, its divine concept or form, not just an impression or representation. Since what is abstracted and known (the process of *adequation*) is not simply what the senses respond to, but rather the immaterial form, the epistemology of conceptual realism is not just empirical. Conceptual realism is not just an idealistic (e.g., Platonistic) epistemology either, for it holds that the abstracted form is actually individuated in the matter as its immaterial principle, and not in the perceiver nativistically.

The concept or form does, however, reside in God, and therefore has a preexistence even before it is particularized (or individuated) in matter. Again, the Catholic understanding of the Creator as a spiritual, nonmaterial being, as pure intellect, mandates the acceptance of a nonmaterial essence (form or soul) in all things. All beings, spiritual or material, exist nonmaterially in the mind of God *in potentia* before they exist actually. Their actual existence then depends on and emanates from their nonmaterial *in potentia* form. Spiritual intellective beings (i.e., angels and men) have forms or souls that are immortal (spiritual) because they are conceived by God as in His image; that is, their form or soul is conceived as either purely spiritual intellectual (as in the angels) or essentially spiritual intellectual (as in man).[5]

The process of abstraction is where the material body of the thing perceived allows man to ascertain its nonmaterial essence. Abstraction is made necessary because of man's limited intellect and his corporality (as compared to the angels). Abstraction can loosely be seen as the reversal of the dynamics of creation: in creating, God first has the idea or essence of a thing in His mind; it has a real spiritual pre-existence. He then creates it materially. The resultant created being then has both spiritual essence and an individual material existence. When man intuits the spiritual essence of a thing (its nature) he once again, as it were, removes it from individual

---

[5] While beings other than angels or man have a spiritual form because they are conceived in the mind of God before they are created or actualized, they are nonetheless conceived by God as purely material beings and thus do not share in His spiritual, immortal nature.

material existence. It is, however, important to note that what man knows is the real individuated being, not the *in potentia* spiritual idea as God knows in the divine ideas.

Epistemological Distortions

Because of man's ability to know essences he can know truth. Even in the Thomistic scheme of things the intellective process is not perfect. There are three main steps to knowing: perception, intellection, and judgment (when the steps of volition are added, the full human act occurs). As mentioned, perception is a physiological process. Aquinas locates its mechanism in the passive intellect, which is material. Man's physical nature and his intellectual dependence (in his earthly state) on material sense perception are due to his limited intellect. It is in physiological perception and judgment—the reasoning process that requires composition and division of ideas—that error can occur. If an object is adequately engaged by the senses then the abstractive process is an infallible intuitive process. There is no error in the abstractive intuition of essence, because error can exist only where there is composition, and in abstraction there is no composition (Sheen 1938, 119).[6]

The greatest source of intellectual error is found in subjectivism, the denial of objective truth. In subjectivism it is the individual's personal beliefs that determine what is true: "What's true for me is true for me, what's true for you is true for you." The pervasiveness of subjectivism is due both to individual personality and characterological flaws and to the ideological denial of truth and its acquisition. The eradication of individual personality and characterological flaws is of the essence of Imago Dei Psychotherapy and will be addressed in subsequent chapters. The ideological denial of truth and its acquisition is the denial of not only the objective but the commonsensical: the everyday belief that a person can discern what is true and what is not. This ideological denial of epistemological commonsense is manifest in the following contrived epistemologies that have such a pervasive influence today.

Eclecticism is the drawing of select ideas from different philosophies. Without internal coherence, there is no possibility of achieving intellectual

---

6 Abstraction, though without error, is not a perfect process; it is limited, for though it intuitively grasps the general idea of a thing, it does not intuitively grasp its particularity.

integrity. Eclecticism, instead of fostering an integrated worldview, requires compartmentalization of thought. This compartmentalization allows for the holding of beliefs that contradict each other. Eclecticism is prevalent among those informed by contemporary popular culture, where "truth" is validated by how one feels about it. Schizophrenia may in a certain sense be conceived as a severe pathological manifestation of eclecticism.

The lack of intellectual integrity that is found in eclecticism is also found in historicism. Here it is not the truth that determines the proper response to the situation, but the situation that determines the truth. Truth is not an eternal mandate but something that morphs to its environment. Again, popular culture or trends determine what is true and good for the person, as opposed to an unchanging natural and divine law. Psychologically, historicism entails a person's abdicating the power to judge freely what is true and good, and submitting to the milieu or peer pressure.

Then there are scientism and pragmatism. Scientism reduces the person to the quantifiable, and thus reduces him to something that can be manipulated. Modern psychological technique is often guided by this false and brutalizing epistemology. Pragmatism, a form of positivism, reduces the good to the functional or successful or popular. Mental health is usually judged purely from a pragmatic point of view. A person's worth is judged by his functionality, his normalcy or sanity in his conformity to group think. Pragmatism holds that what works is deemed to be true.

In the realm of revealed truth there is indifferentism, which is a heresy. Indifferentism views all religions as equally valid. It has manifestations in unbridled ecumenism and in the diminishment of the Church's missionary apostolate. It also manifests itself in a person's compromising values of the faith that are contrary to those espoused in his milieu.

Finally there is nihilism, which is a denial of all truth and, as such, of being itself. It leads to a destructive will to power or to a solitude without hope. Nihilism is often disguised under the auspices of freedom; but without truth freedom is impossible. "The truth shall make you free" (Jn 8:32). The rise of abortion, euthanasia, suicide, and other destructive behavior is a direct result of the rise of nihilism.[7]

---

7 The Protestant Movement in many ways was the beginning of the false epistemological *-isms* that plague the West today. In Protestantism is found the roots of most of these *-isms*: with the Protestant separation of nature and grace it shattered integral

A Catholic clinical psychology, then, has as a fundamental goal the espousal of an epistemology that holds truth as certain and absolute. Psychology must locate itself within an epistemology that has recovered its sapiential dimension, or overarching meaning and directing of life; an epistemology that affirms that the truth can be known, going beyond the empirical, with a metaphysical dimension and horizon.

Knowledge without wisdom is lethal. It is the Church's recognition of truth, as an objective reality that descends from God and transcends man's subjective appreciation of it, that allows her to unite harmoniously the three realms of truth: the quantifiable, the qualitative, and the revealed. Within these three synthesized realms of knowledge all information presented must be harmonized with the truths already assented to be deemed truths. If, sometimes after excruciating examination of both the presented information as well as the already assented to truth, such a harmony is not possible then the information is deemed to be false. Such synthesizing orients one along the straight tangent of the truth, from the empirical, to the logical, to the revealed. The ascent of this narrow path leads to an ever greater vantage point from which the infinite expanse of truth can be viewed, a truth that in Catholicism is seen as integral and harmonious.

Morality: Willing the Good

Truth and good are but differing ways to view being. Being, when considered by the intellect, is truth; when it is desired by the will, it is a good. For man to reach his destiny he must know, love, and serve the truth. Whereas knowing the truth is an act of the intellect, loving and serving the truth/good is an act of the will. Logic allows the intellect to assent to the truth and love allows the will to possess that truth as a good. Once the truth is assented to, there are three phases involved in a volitional act: the desire of the object or good, the intent to acquire that object, and the election to act and to take the means required for acquiring the good.

---

truth and founded modern positivism, eclecticism, and historicism; with its rejection of 1,500 years of constant tradition in favor of individual feelings, values, or inspirations, it laid the foundation for radical subjectivism and immanentism; in its denunciation of the sacral public order it began the movements of nationalism and secularism and planted the seeds of nihilism.

The will's object is always the good; however, the good it chooses is not necessarily the good it should seek. This is the essence of immorality and vice. In a vicious or sinful act a person chooses a lower good (that is, something good in itself, as all being is), but that excludes a higher good. This is the shutting off of oneself to higher goods and ultimately to the highest good, which is God. The moral act, conversely, is one that sacrifices lower goods for higher goods, opening the person up to transcendent values and to God. This openness to the higher good, truth, and value is the hallmark of mental health.[8] It is also the essential dynamics of human existence, the process in which man, who is created for eternal life, ever waxingly chooses that Life in truth and love and thus can become divinized.

Essential, then, to a moral system is its hierarchy of goods.[9] Modern psychology has often proffered its own hierarchy of goods based on its own anthropology and teleology. Abraham Maslow's (1908–1970) hierarchy of goods is the most well known. This hierarchy, which is taught as gospel in public education, makes man's need for God or the transcendent a luxury that is sought only after he has satiated his more essential and hence, by implication, more important needs. In the Catholic schema, God is the highest good. He is essential Being and absolute Truth. Openness, then, to this highest good is openness to being, truth, and reality. In that man is a physical being he has physical needs, but these needs are not more essential to him than his need for God. Indeed, *the satisfying of man's physical needs are goods only insofar as they facilitate his ascent to God.* This is the crucial distinction between a hierarchy of needs (which is the more proper term for Maslow's listing) and the Catholic hierarchy of goods. In a hierarchy of goods one's needs are legitimately met only if they facilitate one's ultimate need of God, who is the ultimate Good. When one chooses to fulfill a need or acquire a good that destroys a higher good or need, then one acts immorally. Indeed, one is called to forgo lower goods in pursuit of higher goods; this is the essence of nobility, heroism, and sanctity; it is the essence of the truly human life. Although man needs to have life and sustenance to function, his functioning should not be ordered to sustaining biological life. The tautological belief that the meaning of biological life is biological life catches man up in a vicious circle that produces a vortex of absurdity and nihilism.

---

[8] See in chapter 6, "Openness-to-Reality."
[9] See in chapter 8, "Hierarchy of Goods."

The will depends on the intellect for its object of volition. The intellect presents the truth to the will as a good (again truth and good are but differing points of view concerning being); however, even though the will depends upon the intellect to present the object as good to it, once the good is willed, the will can in turn influence the intellect by directing it toward further acquirement of the good, or truth, or away from truth, even distorting the intellect's conception of the truth. Such a distortion is intellectual falsity and may be found in a faulty logic that rationalizes evil, or in the ideological raising of a lower good or truth over a higher one, or in the dismissal of a higher truth or good completely. This is why, then, a Catholic clinical psychology must be concerned not only with the intellect, but with the will, for the will is necessary for full acquirement of truth's good and can even cause the intellect to distort its concept of truth. It is the distortion of truth or reality that is the essence of mental illness.

Mental Illness and Moral Culpability

In addition to the spiritual cognitive faculties, man differs essentially from beasts in that he has spiritual volitional faculties. Whereas the intellect's end is the truth, the will's end is the enjoyment of the good. Still, one could say that the will's final or highest end is itself the truth, for truth is being and being is good.

Free will is the engine behind any psychological change. It is the clinician's task to facilitate the therapant's implementation of good will, often in the face of contrary feelings. Those who suffer from mental illness often have a weak will that is led around indirectly by emotions that distort cognitions, rather than a will that is led by right reason and overrides or validates emotions accordingly.

A clinical psychology that denies or downplays the will is one that is only exacerbating the mental ills of its therapants. Imago Dei Psychotherapy recognizes that the strengthening of the will in conjunction with intellectual assent to the truth is the absolute and primary prerequisite for therapeutic success.[10]

While a free choice is clearly definable, it is nonetheless difficult, if not impossible, for a person other than the actor himself to discern the presence

---

[10] See in chapter 8, "The Thomistic Moral Act."

or degree of free will. It is, however, incumbent upon a Catholic psychologist to assume the potential for free choice; indeed, the restoration of the volitional powers constitutes a cardinal goal of Imago Dei Psychotherapy. If one automatically assumes that there is no volitional element to a mental illness, then there is no possibility that a therapy will be devised that could allow for the power of volition to help control or eradicate the illness. Unfortunately, modern psychiatry, and to some extent mainstream professional psychology, appears to assume just that.[11]

The Mandate of Truth

If there is one term, other than those proper names of God Himself, that is central to Catholicism, it is truth. It is in truth that eternal life is found. It is man's very ability to know the truth that makes possible his partaking in salvation, and it is the act of knowing that is his eternal destiny in the beatific vision. Christ states, "And this is eternal life: to know Thee, the one true God, and Jesus Christ whom Thou hast sent" (Jn 17:3). The Second Person of the Trinity is the Word: that is, He is God's eternal knowledge of Himself. The Third Person of the Trinity is the eternal Love that proceeds from the Father and Son's knowledge of each other. Because God is eternal, there is no question of His knowledge of Himself being present without His love for Himself, for His knowledge and love of Himself are simultaneously without beginning.

Once the truth is known, love goes out toward that truth in a certain "ecstasy," which in turn allows further knowledge of the truth, which in turn draws the reality further into oneself. Thus, truth both proceeds and succeeds love, and love is the dynamics. When one loves the truth, he fully embraces the truth. Love then is one's assent and desire for the truth, the culmination of knowing the truth. The quality and ardor of one's love

---

[11] The degree to which a person's free will is diminished by mental illness is one of the most delicate questions in clinical psychology and pastoral morality. However, it can be said with assurance that evil moral choices can lead to and exacerbate pathology, and that most mental illness has its roots in sin, be that sin perpetrated on or by the mentally ill. Nonetheless, to the extent that a person does not freely choose an evil, that is, a lesser good that destroys a higher good, then he cannot be fully culpable for that evil. See in chapter 8, "Vice, Vice Effect, and Inherited Concupiscence."

depends on the validity and depth of one's knowledge. A person must first know something before he can love it, though love can impel him to want to know more about it and thus be enabled to love it even more. Nonetheless, in man's earthly existence charity unites him to the Trinity even more than faith precisely because our faith is not yet (the beatific) vision.

Truth is being; and being, which is reality, is good; thus, *truth, being, reality,* and *good* are all synonyms. He who has being or existence as an essential part of His nature is the highest good. Truth—one's perception of it, one's reflection on it, and one's loving assent to and subsequent acting in conformity with it—then is the destiny of man, and its facilitation is the *raison d'être* of a Catholic clinical psychology. A person possesses truth when he intellectually judges that an object's phantasm (produced by the senses) is in accord with the concept the intellect forms from the abstracted image of the object. This is the comparison of two orders of knowledge: the material/empirical and the spiritual/rational. Truth is also possessed when a person compares a concept to other concepts previously adjudged to be true and finds them harmoniously synergistic. However, it is not until a person wills the truth that he possesses the good of the truth. In possessing the good of the truth, a person goes beyond mere intellectual assent to the truth and wills to love it and act in accord with it. This love and acting in accord with the good is the moral act. Knowing and choosing the highest truths and goods is the noblest love.

Catholicism rises and falls on these epistemological and moral postulates, for without the ability to discern truth with certitude the Church's claim to teach with certitude is meaningless, and without human moral agency—the ability to assent to truth, or do good—man has not the potential for either condemnation or salvation. This is not to say that the gift of faith is not necessary. Here below, reason can lead man only so far. However, knowing that certitude in the natural order is possible makes certitudes of faith plausible.

There are three ways a person can refuse the mandate of the Catholic Church's absolute truth: either he rejects empirical truth and thus lacks the tether of basic experience, or he rejects philosophical truth and thus lacks the link between basic experience and revelation, or he rejects revealed truth and thus lacks the validating endpoint for his line of reasoning.[12] The

---

[12] See Figure 2.1, page 23 in this book.

refusal to accept either empirical, philosophical, or revealed truth allows a person to escape or stray from the narrow and unwavering path they mandate. These three valid and mutually validating modes of knowledge leave no room for man's legitimate dissent.

● ● ●

CHAPTER 5

IDP's Catholic Existential Orientation

Caveat

THE FOLLOWING is as much a criticism of secular existentialism as it is an affirmation of an authentic philosophy of being or existence. Indeed, secular existentialism can be viewed as an apostatic European offshoot of Catholicism. Whether it is possible to authentically combine Thomism and modern philosophical phenomenology in the expostulation of Catholic philosophical and theological truths is at best highly controverted. Phenomenology has its roots in Cartesian subjectivism. Descartes himself, and so his philosophy, was a child of the Renaissance, which was the beginning of Western culture's turn, or return, to a pre-Christian fixation on man.

The error of philosophical phenomenology or secular existential psychology is that it seeks to enter into a person's subjective or internal experience so as to authenticate it. Whereas existential psychological as utilized by Imago Dei Psychotherapy and espoused herein seek to enter into a therapant's internal experience in order to rectify it. Thus IDP does not anchor reality in subjective experience, but rather by entering into the therapant's subjective experience is better able to diagnose and treat his psychological ills, a clinical dynamic that in itself does not exclude the external objective locus of reality as enunciated in Thomism but rather demands it.

As espoused in this treatise, the use of an clinical existential and phenomenological orientation within a Thomistic framework is considered most essential for the clinical science of Catholic psychology. A clinical science must by its method consider phenomena, and clinical psychological science must consider not only the phenomenon of the subject therapant but that therapant's own perception of phenomena. Only after this can the objective norms concerning the human person be applied to remedy the subjective mental state of a therapant, which, again, is first manifested and ascertained phenomenologically. In many ways the ills of modern man, especially his mental ills, are the fruit of man turning into himself. As such, in clinical practice it is imperative that the clinician factor in the subjective, for modern man is deeply ensconced in the subjective, particularly when he is in the throes of mental disorder.

Existence

Existential psychology, like its progenitor modern secular phenomenological-existential philosophy, is most often associated with a secular humanism of subjective morality and teleology, even nihilism. Yet, an existential orientation can, and must, be separated from secular existential ideology. Indeed, an existential orientation can express man's essential yearning for the meaning of existence as the very capacity for objective truth and, ultimately, the Truth. Whereas modern secular existentialism is based on the belief that man's driving search for meaning is futile, an existentialism (that is, a philosophy of existence or being) in harmony with Catholicism holds that this search for meaning is due to an objective teleology that has fulfillment in eternal union with God. The following is as much a condemnation of erroneous phenomenological-existentialism as an affirmation of a *Thomistic philosophy of being and existence*. In addition, the following highlights the need to recognize modern man's mentality—a mentality that is both secular humanistic and subjective—and the place of human encounter in the clinical application of Imago Dei Psychotherapy.

Pope John Paul II (1920–2005) was heavily influenced by modern phenomenological thought and thus his writings are especially pertinent to this discussion. He often began with modern man's subjective fixation on self in his efforts to move him away from self and toward Objective Supreme Being: "The truth comes initially to the human being as a question:[1] *Does life have meaning? Where is it going?* At first sight, personal existence may seem completely meaningless" (1998, no. 26). It is this seeming absurdity of human existence that is used to spur modern man on to seeking tran-

---

[1] This should be understood in an experiential sense, since epistemologically any question must be based in a known truth, for a question is always derived from a truth that appears to need an explanation. However, since the truth that precedes

scendent meaning. Existentialism, seen in this light, is an orientation, a point of departure, a question that can lead to truth and objective meaning. This differs from secular existentialism, which offers the void of the question itself as an end or, more aptly, a dead end.

As a modern movement, secular existential philosophy claims to be a corrective response to the dehumanizing of man that occurs when an ethos ceases to value the search for the meaning of existence and sees man only in a utilitarian way. Specifically, secular existentialism claims to be a response to the advent of industrial, scientific, and technological cultures, that is, to a mindset that does not recognize any knowledge that is not empirical and, as such, does not recognize any elements in man that are not empirical.[2] Secular existential philosophy is said to be a response to the reductive view of the person as only a composite of measurable qualities and his valuation only as an object to be used as a means to an end by political, social, and commercial forces. It is also clearly a reaction to cultural convulse and the ensuing alienation: be it brought on by the demise of ancient regimes, societal upheavals, cataclysmic wars, or moral and domestic revolutions.

In truth the secular existential movement is an unrequited longing for the God and Church from which modern man has strayed. Secular existentialism is not the creation of any one leader, but rather a phenomenon generated by a wide range of thought that has its center in Western Europe, at the very heart of an erstwhile Christendom that was formed by the creative force of Catholicism.

Both the perennial Christian philosophy of Thomism and secular existential philosophy are concerned with the issue of human *being*, that is, of human *existence* (though, as will be seen, while Thomism is ultimately concerned with the pristine being of God, secular existentialism is trapped within subjective self-concern of one's own being). While Thomism asks the question, "What is man?" secular existentialism asks the question,

the questions *Does life have meaning? Where is it going?* is the self-evident truth of existence itself, these questions can be recognized as the beginning of the search for more sublime and urgent truths.

2 Empirical, in this context, refers to that which is a result of efficient and material causality: the quantifiable, segmentable, and measurable. This form of empiricism does not study other forms of causality—the formal and the final—because it does not recognize them as real, an exclusion that is based itself on an extra-scientific or philosophic premise. It is the dominant form of empiricism in science or, more appropriately, scientism.

"Who is man?"; the former is based in objectivity and the latter in subjectivity. Thomism goes further and asks the more essential philosophical questions, "What is being?" and "What is Supreme Being?" addressing the question of man's own being. Still, secular existentialism must be seen as an improvement on technocracy, which asks from a utilitarian perspective, "What is man doing?"

This *being* orientation of both Thomism and secular existentialism requires the uniquely human phenomenon of self-reflection, specifically the ability to reflect upon one's very existence. The ability to reflect upon one's own existence subsequently entails the ability to reflect upon the possibility of one's nonexistence. This dual existential reflection is the most fundamental, sublime, and poignant of all reflective activity. That is why it is said that *all philosophy is a philosophy of death*. To ponder human existence, one's own existence, is to question the meaning of existence. It is this question that is the human question. In the encyclical letter *Fides et Ratio*, John Paul II wrote:

> The first absolutely certain truth of our life, beyond the fact that we exist, is the inevitability of our death. Given this unsettling fact, the search for a full answer is inescapable. Each of us has both the desire and duty to know the truth of our own destiny. (1998, no. 26)

He went on to write, "One may define the human being, therefore, as the one who seeks truth" (no. 28). Such a non-theocentric, humanistic approach, beginning as it does with the experience of post-Christian modern man's subjective existential angst, is by its very secularity ideally suited to engaging that man in the initial stages of psychotherapy; especially since many psychological difficulties are the product of or exacerbated by the West's rejection of the God-centered Catholic ethos.

Thomistic and Existential

Both phenomenological clinical evaluation and the broader modern existential orientation itself, then, at least in clinical psychology, can be conceptualized in a manner that is harmonious with Catholicism. Indeed, it is crucial to do so when seeking to implement an efficacious Catholic clinical psychology. To achieve this utlization, it is the philosophy of St. Thomas Aquinas that recommends itself as the informing philosophy of

Catholic clinical psychology not only because of its unsurpassed Catholicity and systematic thoroughness, but because it is itself an existential philosophy. Indeed, Thomism can be said to be the first truly existential philosophy. K. F. Reinhardt (1952) is here quoted at length as he references this assertion in the works of Armand Maurer and Jacques Maritain, two neo-Thomists of the twentieth century:

> A. A. Maurer . . . points out that St. Thomas inaugurated a real revolution in metaphysics when he turned the philosopher's interest "from form and essence, where it had lingered for many centuries, to the act of existing." It was a decisive moment in the history of metaphysics, he says, "when philosophers became aware of the specific problems which attach to existence as distinct from essence. . . . The Angelic Doctor was the first to recognize the primacy of the act of existing over essence. . . . Even in his youth St. Thomas was regarding being from an existentialist point of view."
>
> Jacques Maritain [who wrote the following early reflections in the wake of his being newly converted to Catholicism], following a similar line of argument, asserts that Thomism is "the philosophy of existence and existential realism." He distinguishes between an "authentic" Thomist and an unauthentic or "apocryphal" philosophy of existence. In the latter category he places all atheistic forms of existentialism. . . . Both "authentic" and "apocryphal" existentialism affirm, according to Maritain, the primacy of existence, but whereas the former preserves essences and thereby the intelligibility of existents, the latter denies essences and thus marks the self-defeat of the intellect and despairs of intelligibility. The French thinker finds the basic error of the atheistic existentialists in their false presupposition that "existence alone is the nourishing soil of philosophy. They treat of existence without treating of being." For the Thomist existentialist (who is a "theist"), on the other hand, essence and existence in the correlation make up the *one concept of being* which analogically, permeates all things as their very act of existing. Being is "that which is" or "that which is able to exercise existence," and at the summit of all beings, in the unity of "Him Who Is," the intelligibility of essence fuses with the superintelligibility of existence. Thus the entire metaphysics of St. Thomas is centered not upon essences but upon existence (228–29).

Catholic clinical psychology can be at one and the same time existential and Thomistic, as is Imago Dei Psychotherapy, which unites a subjective/

inductive/phenomenological dynamic to an objective/deductive/logical metaphysics.

In considering mental health as the ability to *perceive, receive, reflect upon, and act upon the real,* an IDP clinician must take into account both the therapant's subjective experience of "the real" and objective reality itself. For a clinician to acknowledge only objective reality while remaining insensitive to a therapant's subjective experience would be analogous to a physician understanding the principles of physical health while being unable to recognize the symptoms of disease. An effective psychotherapist must first be able to gain the therapant's subjective perspective, to see the world as the therapant sees it, before he can measure the therapant's mental processes and outlook against objective reality.

Clinically, inductive reasoning, with its utilization of phenomenological observation, garners knowledge by noting the therapant's particular symptomology and from it extrapolating general diagnostic conclusions. Deductive reasoning's utilization of logical analysis applies general truths about the nature of man to the particular therapant in order to uncover the etiology of his symptoms. To this end, clinical induction begins with particular symptomology and ends with general diagnostic categorization, while clinical deduction begins with general anthropological principles and ends with particular etiological conclusions. *Together, clinical induction and deduction make possible the compilation of a thorough psychological profile.*

So while a completely deductive clinical psychology would be able to present the objective ideal and goal of mental health, it would be unable to facilitate the therapant's attainment of that goal because it would miss the phenomenon of the person and his subjective experience. On the other hand, a completely inductive clinical psychology does not understand the objective nature of the human person and thus cannot systematically restore a therapant's mental and characterological disorders. Any complete epistemology, clinical or not, must admit of both the inductive/phenomenological process and the deductive/logical process. Induction and deduction are two sides of the same coin and, more often than not, the epistemological process constantly fluxes between the two. The IDP theoretical conceptualization that weds phenomenological existentialism to Thomism assures the integrity of the psychotherapeutic process. Thomism's epistemology of conceptual realism is based on the validity of both inductive/phenomenological knowledge and inductive/logical knowledge, which together produce the complete truth.

It is important to note that the danger of an existentialism without moorings in objectivity is especially grave in psychotherapy. The professionally and popularly dominant humanistic schools, such as those of Rogers or Maslow, are especially apt to exacerbate mental illness or characterological viciousness by their encouragement of radical subjectivity. General secular psychology itself is apt to fall into the pitfalls of an unbridled humanism due to its valid recognition of the need to build therapeutic rapport but its non-assent to philosophically objective truths about the human person.

The Catholic existentially-oriented therapeutic process requires the maintenance of both an authentic subjective rapport between the therapist and therapant, as well as an objective perspective that transcends not only the therapant's subjective view but also the therapist's. It is the Catholic worldview that uniquely provides both: a full appreciation of the unrepeatable uniqueness of each person and the objective standards for human existence.

Analogy of Being

A Catholic/Thomistic philosophy is able to employ both a deductive objectivity and an existential subjectivity because of its recognition of the *analogy of being*. All that exists shares in an analogous way in the existence of God. Of all material beings, man shares most fully in this analogous being, for he shares not only in material existence (as does a rock), or vegetative existence (as does the plant), or sensitive existence (as does the brute animal), but in rational existence, which only God (and the angels) possess. As such, man (like the angels) is properly deemed to be *imago Dei*. This analogous sharing in God's rational existence is also an analogous sharing in God's immortality, for the rational soul is a spiritual soul and, as such is not subject to decay and death. It is only an analogous sharing in God's rational or spiritual being, for only God by His very nature exists; only God is a noncontingent being, a being that cannot not exist.

In that it is essential for God to exist, in God existence and essence are one and the same thing. Not so with man, and this is the crux of his existential anxiety: because of man's spiritual nature he yearns for the noncontingent, yet is relentlessly confronted with his contingency. Man's existential awareness that he need not exist is the greatest of blessings, for if he is responsive it impels him to seek the noncontingent Being upon whom his existence depends.

A Catholic Psychology of Being Equals a Psychology of Truth

Reality, being, truth, and the *good* refer to the same phenomenon, for all are of the essence of God. According to Catholic existential philosopher Gabriel Marcel (1956), "being is what withstands—or what would withstand—an exhaustive analysis bearing on the data of experience and aiming to reduce them step by step to elements increasingly devoid of intrinsic or significant value" (14). In other words, Marcel gives a negative definition that conveys: *go ahead and dissect and segment and reduce and measure as you will and as fully as possible, and that which is not dissectible, that which remains, will be being.* Marcel goes on to say parenthetically that "an analysis of this kind is attempted in the theoretical works of Freud." Freud refused to recognize that there was something that still remained. The empirical scientific (nomological-deductive) method would hold that if something is not analyzable it does not exist. In the final analysis, secular existential psychology, which began in many ways as an answer to the emptiness of scientism and Freudianism, itself finds that nothing exists beyond the distraction that is life.

For secular existential psychology, therefore being becomes a transitory action, a verb devoid of noun status. The secular existential view of the person then is that he is always, or at least should always be, endlessly remaking or rediscovering himself. This view is premised on the belief that there is no essence to be discovered once and for all. The individual does not *find* meaning for his existence by discovering an intrinsic nature or essence, but rather *gives* himself a transitory meaning. Thus there is no essence, but only a *being-in-the-world.* Experience of one's own particular being is quite different. This is the *I am* experience, a belief that one's right to exist and one's intrinsic worth are validated by the mere fact that one (presently) wills to continue to exist.

A Catholic existential view of being and human existence is based on Essential Being, not on man's efforts to create meaningfulness, or his "right to exist," and even less on the subjective will to exist. A contingent being by definition has no right to exist at all; rather, for the contingent being existence is a gift. All being is a sharing in He Who Is, He whose essence is indeed being. Only He Who Is has the "right" to exist.

Existential Teleology

Existential psychology does not hold a theory of personality per se, but rather a theory of the person. Specifically, existential psychology holds a theory of the existing person. At base, this existing person is dynamic and meant for change. The existing person is *one who is*, that is, a being. *Being* in the existential sense is meant as a participle, not a static noun, and connotes the sense of *becoming*. The German word for this existential *being* is *Dasein* (*Da* = there, *sein* = being).

A Catholic existential orientation also acknowledges a dynamic of becoming. This becoming is understood in the light of man's end, for if there is no teleology there can be no rhyme or reason to becoming, there is no way to tell if a person is coming or going, becoming or unbecoming. Catholicism holds that man's teleology is union with God; hence becoming is the dynamic that increases that union. Becoming entails becoming more Christ-like, sanctified, divinized. Growth in holiness, then, is the essential dynamic of becoming, of human growth, and of actualization. (It also entails the "unbecoming" of the pseudo-self, see chapter 7.)

Conversely, secular existentialism is based on a lack of an essential human teleology. Indeed, it is a lack of teleology that nuances secular existentialism's understanding of the term *Dasein*. *Dasein* also has a sense of the arbitrariness and randomness of life. Much like a piece of clay being thrown from the spinning potter's wheel, existence is seen as a result of "thrownness," except with *Dasein* there isn't even a potter, just a cosmic wheel.

This throwness, meaninglessness, or lack of essential teleology necessarily entails ultimate annihilation, for a meaningless life can have no other end. Hence, the dread of death comes from doubt of human life's transcending meaning and of human existence beyond physical death. Secular existential psychology holds that the *Ultimate Concerns* of death and meaninglessness (as well as *freedom* and *isolation*) are seen as the source of anxiety, and it is the repression of awareness via pathological defense mechanisms of these Ultimate Concerns that causes neurosis. The secular existential psychologist Irvin Yalom (1980) holds that it is self-deception concerning these Ultimate Concerns that is the root of all psychopathology.

Imago Dei Psychotherapy also pinpoints man's essential anxiety as an existential one. However, although a sense of arbitrariness will indeed accentuate anxiety, it is nonetheless an erroneous sense. IDP specifically holds that the essential existential anxiety that is part of the human condition stems from the sense of one's contingency, finitude, and particularity; or, in other words, the sense of one's created nature. This sense of one's contingency is akin to the secular description of the "threat of imminent non-existence." IDP holds that what causes this anxiety is that man is meant for eternal life, has a teleology of immortality, yet is unable by his own powers to gain that eternal life or keep himself in existence.

Theistic versus Atheistic Existentialism

Man's awareness that he need not exist should impel him to seek a non-contingent Being upon whom his existence depends. When necessary, Imago Dei Psychotherapy facilitates the existential conclusion that there must be a noncontingent Being. *It is then not only the awareness that one is contingent that is the fullness of existential awareness, but also the awareness that there must need be a creative Being that is noncontingent.*

The reasonable realization that the material world does not have within itself the property of noncontingency, that is, the ability to exist without being created, forces one to accept that there must be an order completely outside the material order that does have this property of noncontingency and uncreatedness. This full existential awareness, which is attainable through unaided reason, enables a person to recognize humanity's lot in life: the frustrations, vicissitudes, and sorrows, as well as the satisfactions, blessings, and joys. How a person deals with this reality and whether or not he fully embraces it will depend on his worldview and the meaning it imparts.

In secular existential psychology, the meaning and moorings one freely chooses, or wills, are not ultimate meanings (i.e., the meaning of life, for life is ultimately meaningless) or objective moorings (moral or otherwise). One finds instead "engagements" that give transitory meaning to one's life and allow one to be unburdened from contemplation of the Ultimate Concerns. Secular existential psychology holds that wholehearted engagement in any of life's activities is intrinsically enriching and temporarily alleviates the inherent dysphoria (but not necessarily the anxiety) by allowing one to pattern the meaningless and unassembled brute data of existence into a coherent, but artificial, whole. Secular existential psychology's Ultimate Concerns cannot be eliminated, only accepted and assuaged.

According to Yalom (1980), "A sense of meaningfulness is a by-product of engagement. Engagement does not logically refute the lethal questions raised by the galactic perspective, but it causes these questions not to matter" (482). Yet are not these engagements then but distractions, temporary defense mechanisms—even if freely chosen and not neurotic—against the anxiety of Ultimate Concerns? Yalom seems to admit that such defense mechanisms are admissible in regard to meaninglessness, but not for the other concerns: "Death, freedom, and isolation must be grappled with directly. Yet when it comes to meaninglessness, the effective therapist must help his clients to look away from the question" (483). But the Ultimate Concern of death also stems from a lack of meaning, for man's meaning or end is nothingness, a complete annihilation that occurs when one physically dies. When human existence is devoid of transcending meaning, death's searing sting remains. The Ultimate Concern of freedom, too, surely stems from a lack of meaning, for without a personal or cosmic teleology all choices are completely arbitrary. Finally, without meaning there is no intelligent and personal Being from which all men originate, only an impersonal and senseless world that by absurd chance has spewed forth various forms of life. There can only be an essential isolation, for there is no such thing as persons created alike in the image of an intelligent, loving God and meant for communion with Him. Such creatures would lack the capacity and commonality that is required for interpersonal relations that transcend the merely utilitarian and superficial.

Thus Yalom's prescription to look away from meaningless is a prescription to look away from Ultimate Concerns in their entirety. Looking away from "meaninglessness" distracts oneself by entertaining subjective meaning; to lose oneself in subjective meaning is only nihilism delayed. It is also inherently dishonest, for it requires a person to lie to himself. In short, despite being high sounding, secular psychology's *engagements* are merely *self-deceiving distractions.*

The combination of freedom and meaninglessness necessitates secular existential psychology's focus on willing or choosing as the essential true dynamics of life. For without objective meaning, one must supply subjective meaning in order to find the motivation to keep on living and to live fruitfully; and without any moorings or parameters one must provide the path and grounding so as to avoid chaotic dissipation. In secular existential psychology, something becomes meaningful by the mere fact that one chooses it freely. Freely choosing, or willing, entails wishing then deciding. Willing is an aspect of freedom; it represents the passage from responsibility to action. Hence, secular existential psychology properly maintains that willing is not impulsivity where the individual acts promptly on all his wishes and thus avoids authentic wishing by failing to discriminate among those wishes; nor is it compulsivity where the individual is not proactive but rather impelled by subconscious demands that often run counter to his conscious ones.

Willing is also paramount to Catholicism. Indeed, willing, or *volition*, is the second crucial area of IDP's therapeutic intervention. Contra the secular existentialists, human willing derives its mental health and characterological benefits not from the mere fact of the willing, but rather its being a willing of the objective Good. That is, one's will must conform to the will of God; it must indeed be a *loving willing* of the Good that transcends one's *self-interested willing*.

The Church promotes an authentic existentialism that does not end in the nihilism that is inevitable when truth is severed from freedom. Note in the following that Pope John Paul II attacked nihilism, and hence secular existential psychology, on its "neglect of being," even though existentialism proclaims "being" to be its *raison d'être*:

> *Nihilism* is the denial of the humanity and the very identity of the human being. It should never be forgotten that the neglect of being inevitably leads to losing touch with objective truth and therefore with the very ground of human dignity. This in turn makes it possible to erase from the countenance of man the marks of his likeness to God, and thus to lead him little by little either to a destructive will to power or to a solitude without hope. Once the truth is denied to human beings, it is pure illusion to try to set them free. Truth and freedom either go hand in hand or together they perish in misery. (1998, no. 90)

Existential Psychodynamics

Like other psychodynamic personality theories, both Imago Dei Psychotherapy and secular existential psychology espouse a theory of dynamic conflicts. But rather than classic psychoanalysis's libido-versus-reality or objects relations' autonomy-versus-differentiation conflicts, IDP and existential secular psychology view the essence of mental conflict or anxiety as having its locus in man's contingency.

Whereas secular existential psychology holds death to be that which makes life meaningless, IDP holds that death, or the realization of one's contingency, is the sine qua non of faith and hence eternal life. Catholicism views death not as an ultimate end but rather as that which ushers man into judgment and subsequently heaven or hell. Both secular existential psychology (purportedly) and IDP seek to bring a therapant to realize fully and become grounded in the inevitability of death. Whereas a secular existential psychology would see this as the source of an ever-abiding anxious dread and a trapdoor of nihilism, IDP views this realization as the first fundamental acceptance of reality—the springboard for faith and the further assent to truth.

Still, it is at the precipice of the yawning chasm of existence that any authentic philosopher, indeed any authentic Catholic, must stand. Life is either a meaningless absurdity ending in a nihilistic void of annihilation or a mysterious sublimity meant for the expanse of beatific eternity. To be sure, it is by peering into this *chasm of choice* that a person is positioned to take an authentic leap of faith. Whereas the secular existentialist gazes into the abyss and, stricken with fear, is unable to believe and so scampers back to the solid but temporal ground of material distraction, the Catholic existentialist courageously leaps into the abyss, believing in the transcendence of his existence, the meaningfulness of life, and the providence of God. It is the Imago Dei therapist's job to bring the therapant to the existential edge and then, if possible, gently to facilitate his choosing a life of faith over one of masked despair.

The Christian existential experience brings about the realization that one will never die and that the way one lives now has eternal ramifications. Specifically, the Church uses the ultimate concern of existence as a spiritual catalyst for the contemplation of the Four Last Things: death, judgment, heaven, and hell. To die with spiritual regret is the only thing to be truly dreaded, or as Leon Blóy (1846–1917) and others have said, "the only tragedy is not to die a saint." This is opposed to the nontheistic existential experience that, in spite of its initial exhilaration, is a false freedom of thinking that there are no eternal ramification: "Eat, drink, and be merry, for tomorrow we die."

Because secular existential psychology holds personal worth, dignity, and intrinsic value to be self-generated and completely arbitrary, those who are not able to give themselves adequate meaning are quite justified in doing away with themselves. Suicide can be considered the ultimate *Dasein* act: the choice not to be.

Existential Angst

IDP agrees with secular existential psychology's supplanting of libidinal impulses as the source of anxiety with existential concerns. Man is "one who seeks truth," not one solely driven by his sexual instincts. It is a truly human existence to contemplate the meaning of being and nonbeing, of life and death. Man, the wise one *(Homo sapiens)*, is meant to be a lover of wisdom *(philosophia)*. Yet how many people face the existential questions in life? An IDP therapist would agree with Socrates, that the unexamined life is not worth living, or at least not worthy of the human vocation. Still, the existential realities of life, in that they are reality, permeate every facet of man's existence, and hence haunt him unceasingly. If the existential realities are not consciously confronted, if there is an attempt to avoid or ignore them, they will exert an unsettling pressure on man's psyche, thus producing the phenomenon of existential anxiety.

Existential anxiety, or *Angst*, conveys "dread," and "anguish." Interestingly enough, secular existential psychology does not make an exact equation between angst and physical fear; that is, the concern with death is not identical with mere concern with physical death. Rather, existential anxiety is the fear of complete annihilation (Yalom 1980). This fear of a complete annihilation that is different from and even more ominous than physical death has as an unspoken premise: that complete annihilation kills something more than just the body, which further supposes that human existence is something more than the purely physical. If fear of physical pain, which is a species of the fear of physical death, is not a species of fear of annihilation, then the difference between the fear of death and the fear of annihilation is not one of degree or intensity. Fear of annihilation is qualitatively different, something other than fear of physical death. Therefore, the secular existentialists, contrary to their official materialism, must fear the annihilation of a nonphysical (spiritual) dimension which is at the very core of human existence. This is but another example of the residue of Catholicism being present in a philosophy that has sought to purge itself of the faith.

Angst (*angustia* = narrowing, straits)[3] entails a constricting of the soul or heart. But the same existential pangs that give rise to this constriction can also give rise to a contraction akin to those of childbirth, where the uterine muscle contracts painfully so that the cervix effaces or opens up to allow birth. Thus angst may be experienced as negative constriction or a positive contraction that facilitates a person's openness-to-reality, that is, to his assent to the truth and embrace of the good.

Secular existential psychology holds that psychic suffering or anxiety can be either neurotically constricting and morbid or creatively opening and life-giving. Hence secular existential psychology goes beyond the psychoanalytic view that anxiety is the dynamic center of neuroses and holds that it is also the dynamic center of creativity; for creativity, like all engagements, is a reaction to anxiety which itself is a reaction to the Ultimate Concerns. In secular existential psychology then, mental health is not living without anxiety, for living without anxiety represents a radical misrepresentation of reality and a denial of the Ultimate Concerns that press on every man. Rather mental health is properly utilizing this anxiety as the catalyst for creative living.

A Catholic Understanding of Existential Anxiety

The IDP understanding of anxiety goes far beyond the secular existential understanding, for IDP views anxiety as a symptom that needs to be transcended in order to embrace the "ultimate concerns." These "ultimate concerns," can be more succinctly and accurately defined as man's concern with his contingency or createdness: *from dust man came and to dust he shall return*. This contingency, or possibility of nonexistence, is the crucial human concern and the source of existential anxiety because man as a creature created in God's image is made for immortality as well as divine life, yet is unable to secure it on his own accord. Thus the human being is

---

[3] Anxiety may derive from *angustia* = narrowing, straits as discussed in Hans Urs von Balthasar, *The Christian Anxiety* (San Francisco: Ignatius Press, 2000), 85.

the most pathetic of creatures; for he is made for eternal beatitude but not even able to keep himself in existence. In addition, man is weighed down by the flesh which is a constant reminder of his mortality and acutely non-divine status. The blessed angels have not the rotting flesh and the brute animals have not the aspirations or capacity. Indeed, it is man's very capacity for the divine that is the source of his deep existential pain, for a capacity is also an emptiness. Thus, man has an infinite emptiness for he has an infinite capacity for the infinitely divine.

Yet God takes on the nature of this "most pathetic of creatures" and appropriates this "rotting flesh" in the Incarnation thus making man now the most blessed of creatures, the only creature that shares a common nature with God. In his very weakness then man finds his greatest blessing. As such, man is called to embrace this threat to his existence, to embrace his contingency and the vulnerability of corporality. In doing so he embraces the pain rather than trying to anxiously fight it or run away from it. The Church has always encouraged the faithful to contemplate the Four Last Things: death, judgment, heaven or hell. It is the Cross itself, the focal point of the pain, that makes the contemplation of these four last things profitable, even joyful, for it is the Cross that defeats death, expiates the judgment, bars hell, and opens heaven, if only a person embraces it.

The existential threat poses the primary choice to embrace the pain of existence or to run from it; it demands a moral response from a person that necessarily entails either vice or virtue. It is at this point that existential anxiety is first encountered. As man is brought to this chasm of choice he can either accept reality, that is, turn toward God in submission or he can fight reality, that is, turn away from God in rebellion. If a leap into reality (and this is the beginning of faith) is not freely taken, a person must either succumb to despair or scamper back to distractions that temporarily assuage that despair. Such distractions are all that secular existentialism has to offer as a temporary reprieve from despair. The world, the flesh, and the devil offer other distractions and numbing agents as well. In contradistinction, the goal of Imago Dei Psychotherapy is to position a therapant on the chasm of existence and gently encourage the leap that is the only way to enter into the fullness of reality. Such a leap requires leaving behind lesser goods: that is, the very distractions that are prescribed by secular existentialists, hedonists, and other escape artists. When these lesser goods and distractions are consciously chosen to the detriment of higher goods, including and most essentially the good of man's existential reality as a mere creature and utter dependency on God, a person sins.

Aquinas says,

> We are speaking of fear now, in so far as it makes us turn, so to speak, to God or away from Him. For, since the object of fear is an evil, sometimes, on account of the evils he fears, man withdraws from God, and this is called human fear; while sometimes, on account of the evils he fears, he turns to God and adheres to Him. (*ST* II–II, q 19, a. 2)

The existential threat, then, can either be the catalyst for embracing the truth and development of virtue or for denying the truth and the development of vice. At this stage the embracing of the truth is not to be confused with religious faith but with the acceptance of a Being that though beyond comprehension is nonetheless known to be All-Powerful and responsible for existence. Such an acceptance is not yet the faith of religion, revealed or otherwise, for belief in a Supreme Being is mandated by the logic of unaided reason. Nonetheless, this elementary assent to truth is the beginning of faith for it is a leap. A man's acceptance of his own existence's radical contingency and complete dependence on a Being that is totally Other is the realization that he is suspended in, or even freefalling through, midair, with no personal control over his footing in existence. Once the elementary truth of one's createdness is assented to, it is imperative that a man continue to be open to and seek reality. A person cannot remain in the air, as it were, without having a sense of urgency about the nature of God. On the other hand, complacency is a sign that one has scampered back to the *terra firma* of illusionary distractions. A complacent attitude about existence and the nature of God is itself vicious, for it means a person has chosen the contentment of lower goods, of distractions, over the highest good, which is truth. The man who does not seek ultimate truth with his whole heart denies as well his human nature, which at its essence compels him to be a desperate seeker of truth and of God.

As such, the refusal to embrace the existential threat by courageously transcending the intrinsic anxiety of existence leads to vice and subsequently further anxiety. Vicious anxiety plagues the man who has chosen lesser goods to the destruction of higher ones. It requires that a man attempt to deny these higher goods by closing himself off from the fullness of reality. This turning from reality, from God, is at the same time a turning to self. It is thus an act that increases self-love and pride. Reality then becomes not only a threat to one's existence but to one's self-love and pride. Though this self-love and pride (see chapter 7) is not of the essence of man, as is his existential emptiness and contingency, it can become so extensive and habituated that one can easily mistake it for who he is.

To various extents then, vicious anxiety impels the sinful man to deny and escape from reality. For such a man the fullness of reality, light and truth, becomes a source of anxiety, for it threatens his sinfulness: both his self-love and pride and the secondary sins that seek to serve and protect that self-love and pride. God Himself, who is ultimate reality, must be denied and escaped. But it is God's light and truth, which is manifested on both the natural and supernatural levels, that is the antidote to anxiety, for it is He who gives a man the courage to overcome his fear and face the pain of his existence. Benedict XVI said,

> He who 'fears' the Lord is 'not afraid.' The fear of God, which the Scriptures define as the 'beginning of true wisdom,' coincides with faith in God, with the sacred respect for his authority over life and the world. Being 'without the fear of God' is equivalent to putting ourselves in his place, feeling ourselves to be masters of good and evil, of life and death. . . . But he who fears God feels interiorly the security of a child in the arms of his mother: He who fears God is calm even in the midst of storms, because God, as Jesus has revealed to us, is a Father who is full of mercy and goodness. He who loves God is not afraid.[4]

Aquinas succinctly delineates the types of fear,

> Accordingly if a man turn to God and adhere to Him, through fear of punishment, it will be servile fear; but if it be on account of fear of committing a fault, it will be filial fear, for it becomes a child to fear offending its father. If, however, it be on account of both, it will be initial fear, which is between both these fears. (*ST* II–II, q. 19, a. 2)

---

[4] Angelus address, Vatican City, June 22, 2008.

It is the clinician's task to discern at what point the therapant is in his relationship with God and work toward improving that relationship, that embracing of Reality. As is often the case, it is a formidable task to bring a therapant to mental health when he is attempting to deny that which is both the cause and cure of his disorder.

Therapeutic Relationship Factors

Secular existential psychology holds that the *Dasein* awareness—the immediate experiencing of being—is nowhere more important than in the therapeutic relationship. This *Dasein* relationship is a source of content for the therapy. However, it is an *encounter* rather than a psychoanalytical transference; that is, it is a relationship that gives rise, not to reexperiencing a critical psychosexual relationship of childhood, but to developing a unique and authentic relationship with the therapist.

This *Dasein* relationship is the basis of the Psychiatric Phenomenology that sprang from Husserl, which strives to experience the other's being in the manner of a fresh, amazed encounter. To enhance observation of the phenomena of the therapant he is encountered as he is, without deductions being applied, with no preconceived ideas or categorizations, but rather in an inductive manner. This encounter disallows even the categories of subject/object. In order to view the person in a holistic manner, the therapist must see him not as a mere object, but rather as an integral subject and object. The therapist encounters the phenomenon of the *acting* person, a subject who is always a dynamic, creative, willing being, never a mere object to be analyzed in an utilitarian manner.

Daseinanalyse then requires that the therapist and therapant have what Buber termed an I/Thou relationship, where each reciprocally encounters the other as subjects in his own right, and where both invest their entire being in the relationship with the other. Some existential therapists would qualify this relationship, as does Van Kaam (1966): "In the nature of the therapeutic situation, the counselor is the fully matured being capable of total self-giving, while the client remains the being in whom this is still only a possibility. Therefore, the initial counseling relationship is unilateral"(38).

Yet to truly view oneself or encounter another authentically, one must see the person as created in God's image, for this is indeed the essence of being. This ability to see the image of God in man has been infinitely enhanced because God was enfleshed in the image of man. It is this *Dasein-in-Christ*[5] that forms the basis not only of a Catholic clinical psychology's therapeutic relationship, but of all Catholic human relations.

Antidote to Dehumanization

Secular existential psychology initially saw itself as a corrective response to the trends in psychology that held that a person can be broken down into composite parts and can be fully understood when these parts are isolated. Such fragmentation and reductionism is found, for example, in Freudian psychoanalysis, where man is reduced to his unconscious, deterministic libidinal impulses, or in Skinnerian behaviorism, where man is reduced to an abstract measurement of his biological stimuli/response mechanisms. Secular existential psychology's response, then, is to maintain an integral view of the person as opposed to the fragmented or composite view. Indeed, this is the essential principle of secular existential psychology.

Yet, incongruously enough, secular existential psychology as secular accepts the premise of the worldview from which issues the dehumanization of man. This is because secular existential psychology itself does not recognize as objective anything beyond the quantifiable, the segmented, and the observable. Existential psychology's proclaimed corrective response to the modern technological view that all is reducible to the quantifiable is also influenced by this view in its considering all nonquantifiable knowledge and experience as valid and real only for the person experiencing it: if it works (pragmatism) and is "real" for you (subjectivism), fine, whether or not it is real and true.

This inability of secular psychology to divorce itself totally from the modern mindset that it rejects is evident in the writings of Rollo May, the great popularizer of secular existential psychology. May's writings are studded with reference to such Catholic luminaries as St. Augustine and Blaise Pascal, as well as references to Scripture. Nevertheless, he reads it all metaphorically or as subjectively "real" only for the referenced believer. May likes the Catholic existential questions, but not the Catholic theological answers, hence his later preference for Eastern emanation religions.

---

[5] See chapter 10, p. 159.

May rightly attributes the utilitarian view of man, man valued for what he does, and the corollary repression of the issue of being, to a particular malaise of the industrialized, technological West. He voices appreciation of other cultures, especially Eastern cultures, and their concern with the issue of being. But there is a fundamental difference between the Eastern answer of the emanation religions (more exactly the Hindu and Buddhist answer) to the issue of being and the Western answer (more precisely Judeo-Greco Catholic answer). The former seeks to eliminate the *angst* of existence by annihilation of the self into an undifferentiated state of being; the latter seeks to sanctify the self by submitting to the divine, thus reaching the highest degree of differentiation by means of unity with the Infinitely Differentiated.

The difference between an authentic Catholic psychology's existential orientation and secular existential psychology reflects the great divide between the Church and the modern world. The radical subjectivism that is at the heart of secular existential psychology permeates all facets of modern life as well as modern clinical psychology. Recent popes have prophetically charged that modern culture is a "culture of death"; secular existential psychology not only succumbs to this culture in the final analysis, but enshrines this culture's nihilism as the center of existence.

So even though Existential Psychology was offered as a cure for the dehumanizing of man, and specifically for totalitarianism both industrial and political, its philosophy only stokes totalitarianism. The "masses" give "existential" meaning to their lives by espousing a myriad of causes, from fanatical support of sports teams to jingoistic nationalism, from animal rights to abortion rights.

The real cure to the dehumanization of modern man is to be found in that which has been intentionally rejected: it is to be found in Catholic anthropology and the imbuing of modern culture with it. Secular existentialism recognizes the illness but has not the cure: a situation that inevitably leads to nihilism and despair. It is only the salvific salve proffered by Catholicism that heals the existential mortal wound that is man's lot without Christ.

CHAPTER **6**

● ● ●

IDP's Tripartite Conceptualization of Mental Health

IMAGO **D**EI Psychotherapy employs the Aristotelian/Thomistic tripartite conceptualization of the soul to form three zones of mental health. Aristotle, and subsequently St. Thomas Aquinas, conceptualized the immaterial soul as that which informs matter to constitute a specific existing being. These souls (or forms) have different powers that give to existing beings a range of capabilities. The differing powers are manifested in the hierarchy of existing beings, be they inanimate beings (as in rocks), living (as in plants), animated (as in brute animals), or reasoning (as in man).

In Zone III of the tripartite conceptualization of mental health, the *vegetative power* is dominant or typifying; in Zone II the *sensitive power* is dominant or typifying; and in Zone I the *rational power* is dominant or typifying. This tripartite model is described as "typifying" because, while a person's interaction with reality may be characterized by a predominance or marked influence of a particular power, *all three powers are always present,* for these powers are all integral parts of the singular human soul. Thus in man the vegetative is present in the sensitive and the vegetative and sensitive are present in the rational. So too, though the vegetative or sensitive may characterize a person's mental state, they nonetheless always bring into play, even if in a reduced and subservient manner, the higher faculties of the soul.[1]

---

1 Aquinas also utilized a conceptualization of the soul that recognized five powers of the soul: the vegetative, the sensitive, the appetitive, the locomotive, and the rational. Both the tripartite and five-power models are based on the functional levels of living organisms. But because man's soul is an integral whole, which renders any divisions an artificial construct, and because it is deemed more facile for clinical conceptualization, the tripartite typifying model is herein utilized. Again, further

Tripartite Corresponding Continuums of Mental Health

Five corresponding continuums (see Table 6.1) are categorized in accord with the typifying powers of vegetative, sensitive, and rational. The first continuum is *openness-to-reality*, which is the touchstone of mental health and is a direct elaboration on the pertinent psychological aspects of the tripartite typifying powers. The next three continuums, *cognition, volition,* and *emotion,* are sub-powers or faculties of man that emanate from the three typifying powers and are crucial to his mental health.[2] As with the tripartite typifying powers categorization, the continuums of openness-to-reality, cognition, volition, and emotion are based on Thomistic conceptualizations. The last continuum is *clinical descriptors* which correlate classifications used by modern psychology with the previous Thomistic continuums.

Openness-to-Reality

The second continuum, openness-to-reality, is a further elaboration on the typifying powers' realm of engagement. IDP maintains that mental health consists in a person's correspondence to the real: in correctly perceiving reality, appropriately interacting with it, and effectively manipulating it. Openness-to-reality measures the degree to which a person accepts and embraces the human experience that is proffered to him.

Openness-to-reality also identifies a person's degree of self-centeredness. Not only is "self-centeredness" (or "selfishness") a universal pejorative and the most common descriptor of a flawed character, it is also a crucial factor in the etiology and remedying of mental illness. Fixated self-centeredness, that is, radical egocentrism, universally characterizes the mentally ill.

---

describing the tripartite model as "typifying" emphasizes the integrity of the soul even though one power is predominately influential. So too, in accord with the integrity of the soul, that which would traditionally be seen as relegated to a higher power in the five-power model is also seen as present in the lower powers in the tripartite typifying model. Thus the tripartite typifying model's vegetative includes much of the sensitive, and the sensitive includes much of the appetitive (locomotion is only indirectly relevant to psychology).

2 Thomists often use the terms *powers* and *faculties* interchangeably. For sake of clarity herein, "powers" refers to the larger tripartite abilities of the soul (vegetative, sensitive, and rational). "Faculties" refers to those more specific abilities of the soul that Aquinas discovered as emanating from one of the tripartite powers, especially those facilities that emanate from the rational power.

Table 6.1
IDP'S Tripartite Corresponding Continuums of Mental Health

Zones	III	II	I
Typifying Powers	Vegetative	Sensitive	Rational/Spiritual
Openness to Reality	Fixation on Bodily Sensation; Disengaged from Reality	Fixation on Material Objects; Personality Distorts Reality	Open to all Reality; Able to Breach Defenses
Cognition	Processing Distorted/ Reflection Minimal; Completely Subjective	Reflection Distorted; Subjectivity over Objectivity	Minimal Distortion; Objectivity Dominates
Volition	Chooses Goods of Visceral Sensation	Chooses Goods that have Subjective Value	Chooses Goods because of Objective Value
Emotion	Visceral Emotions of Pain and Pleasure Debilitate Reason and Volition	Binding Emotions of Sadness and Glee Override Reason and Volition	Marshaled Emotions of Sorrow and Joy are Ordered to Reason
Clinical Descriptors	Psychotic/Axis I	Neurotic/Axis II	Insightful/Functional

This does not, however, automatically impute guilt, for such radical ego-centrism is characteristic of small children, and some of those with mental illness may also lack the requisite reason or volition for culpability. Yet in most cases, radical egocentrism is a form of pride and self-love, for it arises from seeing oneself as the center of the universe and thus entails a certain contempt of others.[3]

That openness-to-reality is not equivalent to a person's organic ability to perceive distinctly all the facts of reality, but rather to the ability to encounter fully the reality he is presented with or is capable of perceiving. Hence there is not a necessary correlation between mental retardation and mental illness.[4] It is not so much the *definitiveness* of perception but rather the *breadth* and *depth* of perception, the full experiential range of human existence from the tragic to the triumphant, that is the hallmark of mental health. Indeed, it is axiomatic that those who lack some degree of open-ness to empirical sensation or intellectual processing because of organic deficiency seem more fully open to transcendent realities, and to God Himself, and thus manifest a sort of *autistic-mystic-savant* syndrome. Childlikeness is a requirement for heavenly residence, and God may choose the "foolish to confound the wise."

Openness-to-reality entails both precognition and cognition. The pre-cognitive entails an existential awareness and subconscious disposition that when impaired diminishes a person's openness-to-reality. A person who is unable or unwilling to stand outside himself and view his subjec-tive experience objectively is unable to have existential awareness.[5]

---

[3] See in chapter 8, "Hierarchy of Goods," and in chapter 9, "The Silver Bullet of Psychotherapy."

[4] However, because of the negative interpersonal relationships and maladaptive socialization of those with mental retardation, they have a high prevalence of dual diagnosis (mental retardation and mental illness). For those with mental retarda-tion, the lack of deep interpersonal relationships and the stress or incomprehensi-bility of the modern milieu's requirements of complex functionality can lead to some form of personality disorder. The *DSM-IV* emphasis on the criterion of functionality as an indicator of both mental health and normal intellectual func-tioning makes a dual diagnosis almost inevitable. For more on the criterion of functionality, see in chapter 3, "The Teleology of Secularism."

[5] See in chapter 7, "The Defense of Personality."

Cognition

Openness-to-reality also entails conscious cognition. Cognition is a function of the intellective faculty and is a further Thomistic delineation of the rational typifying power of the soul. The intellective process involves perceiving, processing, and reflecting upon the real or truth;[6] it is that which makes man rational.

Cognition entails manifold intellective subfaculties and as such is not as distinct or simple as the present categorization conveys. However, this categorization does suffice to convey that which is of immediate therapeutic import: that the person whose faculties of the soul are all being actualized operates on the fully rational level. This fully rational level entails the ability to abstract or universalize.[7]

Imagination plays an important part in intellection; it is also a key factor in mental illness. Aquinas says that imagination makes it possible for a person to know something that is no longer physically present, which allows the use of previous knowledge.[8] Imagination also makes possible creativity, where a person works with and refashions objective reality in a manner congruent with that reality. But imagination is a two-edged sword, for it also makes possible the creation of a subjective "reality" that is noncongruent with or is a denial of objective reality. Imagination can activate the emotions to as great an extent with subjective "reality" as it can with objective reality; indeed, in the mentally ill subjective "reality" overrides objective reality.

The Imago Dei conceptualization of mental health requires that cognition, or the intellective faculty, have place of primacy. A necessary anthropological prerequisite for any Catholic clinical psychology is holding that the intellective nature of the soul is man's specific difference and separates him from the rest of material creation, for it is his spiritual, indeed immortal, element. So while the vegetative and sensitive are unable to exist without matter (without material existence), the intellective is. For the Catholic clinician, this immortality of the soul is obviously not a negotiable principle,

---

6 In IDP the term *reflection* or *reflecting upon* refers to the Thomistic technical term of *judgment*.

7 For an explanation of abstraction, see in chapter 4, "The Spiritual Nature of Intelligence and Knowing."

8 Imagination also plays a more fundamental role in presenting all knowledge to the agent intellect for abstraction (*ST* I, q. 84, a. 7).

and so a Catholic clinical psychology is vehemently opposed to the widespread belief in the scientific community that mind equals body.

Volition

Volition, the faculty of the will, acts upon concepts when those concepts are presented to it by the intellect as something desirable. Volition, like the emotions, is an appetite. But unlike the passions, it is not a physical appetite and is not moved by the sensible; rather it is moved by the intellect. The faculty of the will depends upon the intellect to present it with the good. The intellective faculty grasps a truth and presents it to the will as the good. Yet the will not only is passive, but can influence the intellect by choosing to pursue a particular good.[9] Because the will (unlike the emotions) is not inclined toward any one particular good, it has the capacity of *choice*, the capacity to incline or disincline toward some good and to one good over another.

Volition entails morality, for the sinful act is essentially a volitional act of choosing a lower good over a higher one. Repeated improper choices begin to affect cognition by blinding one to the higher truths/goods that are destroyed in the sinful act. In such cases, it is usually the visceral (bodily) and subjective goods of the emotions that are chosen over and to the destruction of higher goods known by reason. In such a case, the intellect and will are described by Aquinas as being *bound* by the emotions.

It must be noted that to address these moral issues in the current climate of mental health is taboo. Not only is there an antagonism against traditional moral constructs and an emphasis on egoistic enhancement, but the consumeristic orientation of the profession, where the patient or therapant is considered a "client," avoids that which is too unpleasant to that client, and especially avoids anything that might sound like a condemnation of lifestyle. However, immorality and self-centeredness—indeed sin and the demonic—are intrinsically linked to and are a precipitator of mental illness.[10]

---

[9] When the will chooses a particular concept as the good it desires, the intellect is again called into play to focus on that good and in turn again presents that concept with accentuation to the will. Thus intellect and will influence each other.

[10] These moral designations are not meant to be definitive judgments, nor should the designation of *immoral* be accompanied by any disdain for the therapant; rather these moral designations are intended to facilitate a therapist's work in effecting

Cognition and Volition Equal the Moral Act

A person's moral state depends on whether or not he is disposed or habituated toward choosing the good. Virtue is "a habit perfecting a man's will and lower appetites to dispose him to act in accordance with right reason" (Attwater 1961, 518). Thus, when cognition, or the intellective faculty, has full openness-to-reality and has a clear sight-of-the-truth, and volition, or the will, strives for the good in the steadfast service of cognition, and the emotions, or appetitive faculty, are under the sure discipline of the will, a man is habituated toward choosing the true and good and is called virtuous.[11] An Imago Dei therapist helps a therapant first develop the disposition toward choosing the good as the means of developing a habit of choosing the good.[12]

A person can reject the general good in view by focus on a lesser aspect of it (that is, on a particular lower good to the exclusion of a higher good), and if this is done habitually, it can actually cause the willful rejection of the good to impair his view of that good and thus diminish his openness-to-reality. While a person's cognitive assent to the truth is not always a product of volition or moral choices (i.e., there may be organic abnormalities), his morality is always based on cognitive assent and volition, no matter how limited that assent and volition may be. This is because the moral act is by definition a rational and volitional choice of a good.

When being is spoken of as an object of the intellect it is called reality; when it is spoken of as an object of the will it is called the good.[13] When the intellect's understanding coincides with reality there is truth. When the will's object coincides with the good there is virtue or morality. Being virtuous or moral is not simply following a set of rules (indeed, it at times

---

the needed change in a therapant. In any case, a therapist must always keep in mind certain pastoral proverbs espoused by the Holy Church: all men are sinners; a person should be most acutely aware of his own sin and thus see himself as the most egregious of sinners; appearance or self-reports do not always reflect the presence or absence of sin; and one is charged with loving even the most egregious of sinners while hating the sin.

[11] These key elements of the human/moral act—openness-to-reality, sight-of-the-truth, striving-for-the-good—are discussed in chapter 8.

[12] The cardinal moral virtues and the place of inculcating the virtues are outlined in chapter 8, "Realm of Practical Functioning."

[13] Though IDP uses "reality" to designate the object of the intellect, the object of the will, the good, is also the real.

may mean breaking conventional rules); rather, being moral consists in being responsive to and acting in accord with reality. Morality is thus dependent on objective reality, just as the will is dependent on reason.[14]

The cognitive and volitional faculties are specifically that which make man man and constitute the elements of the fully human or moral act. The inclusion of Thomistic cognitive and volitional elements of the moral act safeguards against the tendency to rule out free agency or moral culpability when mental illness is diagnosed. As will be seen, the presence of mental illness does not exclude volition as an etiological factor, but, to the contrary, indicates that volition is indeed impaired.

Emotion

Emotions or passions are generated by the appetitive faculty. Man to an extent shares emotion with animals, though emotion is moved for each through different faculties. In man the faculty that moves the passions is the cogitative, and in animals it is the estimative. When the cogitative faculty is used merely to associate a previous pleasure to an object it functions on the level of the estimative power in animals. However, a man's emotions or passions can also be moved by reason, even to the point of overriding sense stimuli, such as when a man acts courageously in the face of fear.

The human emotional power or the appetitive faculty is divided into concupiscible and irascible emotions, both of which are further divided into positive and negative emotions. Concupiscible positive emotions are love, desire, and delight, and their respective contraries are the negative emotions of hate, flight, and loss (sorrow). The concupiscible appetite is attracted to that which gives sensible pleasure and repulsed by that which gives sensible pain. The irascible positive emotions are hope and audacity, and their respective contraries, despair and fear, as well as anger, which has no contrary, form the irascible negative emotions. The irascible appetite is inclined to overcome contraries and rise above obstacles in accord with the concupiscible appetite's desire or repugnance toward a thing.

Emotions are of different qualities or levels depending on their object; these levels range from the superficial to the profound. Imago Dei Psycho-

---

[14] Though reason and will have a circular relational dynamic, at the very highest point of this dynamic reason is logically "prior."

therapy uses the term *visceral emotions* when the object of the emotions is primarily physical sensation, as is the case of a person in Zone III. Visceral emotions are equivalent to the above-described estimative emotions of nonrational animals. In sum, a person who is fixated on visceral emotions is dominated by physical *pain* and *pleasure*,[15] be that pain or pleasure produced by external stimuli or by the imagination.

When the object of the emotions is a person's subjective good, overriding reason and distorting objectivity, they are termed *binding emotions*. Binding emotions are found in a person whose feelings, both physical and psychological, determine his actions. Binding emotions override reason and distort objectivity to such an extent that they are detrimental even to the subjective good the person seeks. A person who is fixated on binding emotions is dominated by the totally self-oriented emotions of *sadness* (self-pity) and *glee* (self-gratification).[16]

When the emotions are subjected to reason they are termed *marshaled emotions*. Marshaled emotions are those that either are congruent with reason or are subjected to reason. A person with marshaled emotions may still seek his subjective good above all else; however, he is able to use reason to achieve that good and objectivity to measure it. The extent to which a person assents to objectivity and marshals his emotions will determine the profundity of his *sorrow* and *joy*, that is, his openness to the vicissitudes inherent in human existence.

Thus it is the object of the emotions that determines their moral quality. The object of the emotions is the good they seek and love. The emotions are proper and profound (marshaled) when their object is proper and profound.[17] They are improper and superficial (visceral or binding) when their object is improper and superficial.

Though the morally correct act is also totally reasonable, a person may employ reason and volition to a high degree in seeking an improper end, in loving a good to the exclusion of a higher good. A person may appear to be

---

[15] For a detailed description of the three levels of emotionality (pain-pleasure, sadness-glee and sorrow-joy), see chapter 9.

[16] IDP employs the term "glee" as the opposite of "sadness" as per its definition as "jubilant delight" and its derivation from the Old English *gliu* which conveys "entertainment, mirth, and jest." Glee thus can designate enjoyment that is hyperactive, superficial, and self-centered.

[17] See in chapter 7, Figure 7.1. Love-Based Emotions.

fairly well ensconced in Zone I of marshaled emotions, but still be immoral.[18] In such a case a person has idealized or spiritualized his self-love.[19]

Clinical Descriptors

The last continuum, *clinical descriptors,* utilizes the mental health profession's conceptualization of mental disorders and includes the clinical categorizations of both the traditional psychodynamic model, with its focuses on underlying causes, and the medical/psychiatric model, with its focuses on overt symptomology.

The traditional psychodynamic conceptualization of psychological disorders utilizes a continuum model where psychoses and neuroses are, respectively, greater and lesser mental illness, differing in quantity of illness but not quality. The *DSM* descriptor is based on the *Diagnostic and Statistical Manual.* Unlike a psychodynamic model, the *DSM* medical model does not conceptualize mental health on a continuum but divides psychological maladies into distinct categories of Mental Disorders (Axis I) and Personality Disorders (Axis II) and is loath to see a relation between the two. Nonetheless, the *DSM-III* Axis I (Mental Disorders) and Axis II (Personality Disorders) classifications greatly correspond to the traditional psychodynamic psychotic and neurotic classifications from which they evolved.

Whereas the traditional psychological or psychodynamic conceptualization is concerned with not only symptomology but with etiology or causation, the psychiatric conceptualization is concerned primarily with symptomology.

> There are two major approaches to diagnostic psychopathology. The first is called the *descriptive* [medical or psychiatric] because diagnoses[20] are based on relatively objective phenomena that require nominal clinical inference; these phenomena include signs, symptoms, and natural history. The second is called the *psychological* [psychodynamic] because diagnoses are based primarily on inferred causes and mechanisms. The psychological approach also considers descriptive phenomena, but as . . .

[18] See below, "Caveat: Mental Health Is Not Spiritual Health."
[19] See in chapter 7, "Functionality and Pathology."
[20] Insofar as the medical model (descriptive or psychiatric) does not make clinical inference but only describes and seeks to alleviate symptomology, it must remain, strictly speaking, nondiagnostic.

manifestations of more profound underlying forces. . . . The descriptive approach focuses on the what of behavior, the psychological on its why. (Maxmen and Ward 1995, 8)

The psychological/psychodynamic primarily seeks to treat a therapant's intangible psychological influences by means of psychotherapy, whereas the psychiatric/medical/descriptive primarily seeks to alleviate a patient's symptomology, including physiological imbalances, by means of the administration of drugs.

Zone III

(A person is said to be within the following zones when he is at the time predominately or habitually so disposed. This means that there may occur overlap between the zones. A person who is characteristically in Zone II may experience an emotional crisis that results in his falling into Zone III, or a person who is characteristically in Zone I may occasionally lapse into Zone II behaviors under stress.)

Typifying Power: In Zone III, the vegetative power predominates. This does not mean that a person is in a "vegetative state," where the sensitive and rational powers are organically prevented from manifesting themselves, but rather that the vegetative power is utilizing the higher powers for its own ends. Zone III mental illness to some degree entails a physical fixation on one's bodily and emotional sensations. This physical fixation can be seen as a regression to an *infantile hedonism*, where a person is reduced to a primordial engagement with reality.

Openness-to-Reality: When the Zone III vegetative power dominates, a person's openness-to-reality is severely constricted. The person is fixated on bodily sensations and mental rumination (via imagination) and thus unable to view objectively these sensations and ruminations. For example, moods, such as feelings of depression, mania, or anxiety, will become dominant and all-encompassing and thus become disorders. Neither objective truth nor even a rational self-interest prevails, but rather physical feelings. Thus the most mundane and visceral subjectivism determines "reality."

Cognition: In Zone III, the intellective process is severely distorted. Reflection is minimal or so radically distorted via imagination that the very sensing or processing of reality is warped. This is the realm of delusions and hallucinations. In this realm a person *in practice* functions on the level of *subhuman process*. The cogitative faculty (that power which moves the emotions) dominates and is used like the estimative faculty of animals to merely associate a previous pleasure or pain to an object. Though a person in Zone III may still employ the intellect to a high degree, the intellect is nonetheless at the service of the lower passions, be these, for instance, the fears of the paranoid person or the concupiscence of the depressed person.

Volition: In Zone III, a disordered appetite and an untethered imagination distort reason, and thus volition becomes, in effect, a weak, subservient agent of the visceral emotions. With the absence or diminishment of either reason or volition an act cannot be a fully human act. As such, it is not a truly or fully moral act,[21] and thus a person in Zone III is seen as *overtly* amoral. However, the overt manifestation does not necessarily equate with the actual internal disposition. Also, note well that the present amoral state is the culmination of previous immoral actions. Nonetheless, it can be said that in most cases the gravity of a person's psychological impairment proportionally reduces his *present* moral culpability,[22] and even reduces him to a pre-moral state, equivalent to a child's state before the age of reason, where at least theoretically, grave sin is impossible.

Emotion: In Zone III visceral emotions dominate, and a person is fixated on his physical sensation, be it pain or pleasure. These dominant visceral emotions can be either concupiscible or irascible, negative or positive.

In Zone III, when the negative concupiscible appetite dominates and the irascible appetite is weak, a person experiences major depression.[23] Here a person is no longer reacting angrily to suffering (which would be the case if the irascible appetite were stronger), but is reacting to negative stimuli in a

---

21 See chapter 8.

22 This does not exculpate a person from previous immorality that may well have led to the present condition of mental illness, and it is the remedying of that previous immorality that gives rise to the most positive prognosis.

23 The negative concupiscible emotions, hatred, flight, and loss, are here joined by despair, which is traditionally considered a negative irascible emotion. Unlike the other irascible emotions, despair does not move one to overcome obstacles, but rather is the absence of hope, a positive irascible emotion. For a full description of the emotions, see chapter 7.

radically passive way. Paradoxically, a person in such a depressive state may actually exacerbate his depressive feelings or pain to have the "pleasure" of feeling at all. A person in Zone III will have the concupiscible desire for tangible goods but not the irascible passion to attain them, especially when there are obstacles. At times even concupiscence is barely manifest, as in the case of the catatonic schizophrenic. But even here it has been shown in clinical studies on behavioral modification that catatonic patients are still responsive to the most mundane physical rewards, such as candy, and as such are still impelled by the concupiscible appetite, as mundane as it may be.

In service of the concupiscible, the irascible appetites may also be violently present in a person in Zone III. When this is the case, the result may be one of, or a combination of, manic, obsessive-compulsive, paranoid, and psychotic behaviors. For example, those in Zone III may be recklessly driven to pursue visceral pleasures in sexual activities or substance abuse, or their lives may be completely dominated by unfounded fears, obsessions, or compulsions, or they may attempt to perform actions and obtain ends far beyond their ability, or they may be so extremely dominated by their visceral feelings that even objective reality is expected to or believed to conform to those feelings.

Clinical Descriptors: In Zone III of the psychodynamic descriptor reality testing is to some degree impaired. In accord with the IDP psychodynamic premise that psychoses have part, most, or all of their origins in characterological factors, the turning away from reality because of trauma or habitual and obsessive neurotic conversions may result in a psychotic conversion, lapsing from Zone II into Zone III. It is here that is found the most severe grade of mental illness: extreme psychosis where a patient is totally out of touch with reality. A psychodynamic description would categorize those falling within this zone as psychotic.

The psychiatric medical model of the *DSM* categorizes those who fall within Zone III as Axis I (Mental Disorders). The contemporary medical profession of psychiatry views Zone III, or Axis I, disorders as organically based and treats such disorders with psychotropic medications. Even psychoses and severe mood disorders may well be the result of, or activated by, a radical egocentrism; and they are surely exacerbated by it.

Zone II

Typifying Power: The sensitive power predominates. Here the sensitive differs from the vegetative in that a person is more ordered toward the reality that transcends his own subjective bodily experience. He has a sense of objective reality, although that reality is still limited to what physically and emotionally impacts his person.

Openness-to-Reality: The person is fixated on material objects as they impact his person. He partakes in only partial reality or sees reality in disproportion because it is measured by his subjective desires or repulsions. This zone entails errors of logic that are often caused by the overriding of reason by the passions. Thus mental illness in Zone II entails to some degree a fixation on material beings. Such a state can be labeled functional materialism, where all the faculties of the soul are ordered toward fulfillment of a person's subjective needs, both physical and emotional.

Cognition: In Zone II, objective reality is still distorted because it is dominated by the subjective. This subjectivity hampers abstraction of the intellective process or the ability to take a transcendent or objective point of view. A person in Zone II is radically subjective and unable to stand back from his own experience. Though the intellect in Zone II is cognizant of the objective, it is primarily fixated on the material object that stimulates sense and emotional gratification. The material object need not be physically present but may be present through the imagination.

In Zone II a person is still egocentric, but he can partially see how his actions impact others. However, the Zone II person's concern with an action's impact on others stems primarily from a concern with how this will eventually impact himself. A person in Zone II is often a master at manipulation. The classic example of the self-centered and manipulative personality is that of the borderline personality.

Volition: In Zone II, a person demonstrates full use of his will and reason at the service of disordered appetites. A person chooses to do the bidding of his emotions in defiance of reason and to the detriment of what he knows are higher goods. Volition is bound by emotions rather than guided by reason. As such, a person in Zone II is viewed as fully culpable for his actions and thus characterized as immoral. Sinful acts are human/moral acts that are perverse. They are disordered acts that utilize reason. If reason were not utilized, they would not be sins, for they would entail no moral culpability. The perversity lies in subordinating reason to passion or in violating reason by the destruction of a higher good/truth in favor of a lesser good/truth.

Emotion: In Zone II, a person experiences binding emotions where his physical and psychological feelings bind both reason and volition. Whenever the rational faculty is dominated by the emotions, a person views reality from the perspective of his own egocentric emotional interests; truth becomes subjective. In short, a person in Zone II acts in accord with either sadness or glee, that is, with feelings of either self-pity or self-gratification. In Zone II, the irascible appetite is always influential, but since self-interest is still the arbitrator of reality and volition, it serves the self-interest of the concupiscible appetite. The influence of the irascible appetites allows a person to pursue more than just the most mundane of physical and emotional goods (specifically, the irascible appetites allow him to interact with others) even if it is an arduous undertaking. Characteristically such interaction is of a manipulative nature, since radical egocentricity and self-interest are the engines behind such interactions.

In Zone II, the emotions—love/hate, desire/flight, delight/loss, hope/despair, audacity/fear, and anger—are ordered toward the subjective desires of a person, to the detriment of objectivity. Such an orientation can cause enormous psychological disorder and great interpersonal chaos.

Clinical Descriptors: In Zone II is found mental illness that is traditionally and psychodynamically described as neurotic or characterological. Here a person is in touch with a reality that is distorted. Repeatedly choosing not to act in accord with the mandates of reality results in what may be termed *neurotic conversion,* lapsing from Zone I and becoming habituated in Zone II. The *DSM* categorizes those who fall within Zone II as Axis II (Personality Disorders). However, axis I disorders, such as depression, may also be found in an attenuated form in Zone II. This discrepancy is due to the *DSM*'s erroneous belief that mental disorder does not admit of a broad continuum of mental disorders that easily traverses Zones III and II and can even be discerned in Zone I.

Zone I

Typifying Power: The rational power is predominating. The rational power is the spiritual power; it is that which allows abstraction, differentiating man from other sensate animals.

Openness-to-Reality: In Zone I, a person is open to all realms of reality, including that of the spiritual. Spiritual here refers not only to nonmaterial reality but to the ability to consider material reality objectively and then to transcend it. The rational or spiritual power allows man to stand outside himself, to transcend his subjective experience and material reality and thus be able to reflect upon himself and his existence objectively. This level of openness-to-reality makes possible but does not necessitate an openness to the ultimate reality, God, or an openness to others that is fully empathetic.

In Zone I a person is habitually disposed to the acceptance of all three realms of reality. Although placement in this zone indicates a functional openness to all reality, to the degree that a person acquires an *existential awareness* is the degree that he traverses the full extent of this zone. However, it is postulated that the majority of people today do not consider the ramifications of existence, an endeavor more ascribed to the exceptional classes of authentic poets and philosophers. But finally it is only those, rarer still than poets and philosophers, who acquire a mystical awareness that fully traverse and then transcend Zone I's openness-to-reality. It is the authentically pious and the saints who are the purviewers of the mystical, who begin to glimpse reality's endless expanse that is the beatific vision.

Cognition: In Zone I the predominate intellective process is *spiritual cognition.* In this realm, reason predominates, both in a person's universalizing ability and in his logical thinking. As such, it entails a person's objectivity, standing outside self-gratification; even if it is only a self-centered delayed gratification; that is, it allows assent to the truth even when that truth is painful or detrimental to a person's perceived or immediate self-interest. A person may still have a limited, tainted, or erroneous vision of the truth or ideal, such as is the case of the espousal of an unjust or evil cause or the seeking of one's own glorification (see chapter 9, *Idealized Self-Love*).

In Zone I, cognition is positioned to be perfected by the intellectual virtues,[24] culminating in the acquisition of wisdom.

Volition: In Zone I a person's volition is in the service of his reason, and his appetitive faculty is to a large extent controlled and molded by the intellective faculty. A person in Zone I is habituated to acting in accord with reason and by varying (but not necessarily Catholic) standards may be considered moral or virtuous. Volition is usually strong enough to act in accord with reason regardless of the immediate influences of the emotions. Either emotions are congruent with reason (what one loves is what one ought to love and thus volition is fueled by these emotions), or volition is strong enough to act in accord with reason regardless of the contrary influences of the emotions.

In Zone I volition is positioned to be perfected by the moral virtues, namely, prudence, justice, fortitude, and temperance.[25] If cultivated, these moral virtues ensure that reason orders the appetites rather than the appetites order reason. However, the high development of certain moral virtues can be present in a man who is intensely, even demonically prideful.

Emotion: In Zone I marshaled emotions dominate. A person is able to feel both sorrow and joy; he is able, to some extent, to accept the objective vicissitudes inherent in human existence. All the emotions are present, both concupiscence and irascibility, but, unlike the case of the person in Zone II, they are ruled by reason or the cognitive faculty via the will. The dominance of the cognitive over emotion is habitual and redefines, realigns, and refines the emotion's objects of desire.

Clinical Descriptors: Zone I is the realm of mental health. Although this realm of mental health admits of its own gradations, it is characterized by an overall openness to all reality and always allows for *free exercise of volition in accord with the mandates of reality, even if that option is not always chosen.*

---

[24] The intellectual virtues are *understanding*, (which grasps first principles immediately) *science* (which is the formal inquiry into the nature of things), and *wisdom* (which considers the highest causes and judges and orders all knowledge).

[25] See in chapter 8, "Realm of Practical Functioning."

Caveat: Mental Health Is Not Spiritual Health

Love is the ultimate volitional act, and in Zone I love of the highest goods is made possible. Note well, however, that it is not necessitated and that the vice of pride and self-love can still remain. This pride and self-love can be fueled by the very fact of a person's mental health, functionality, talents, and other virtues. A person firmly ensconced in Zone I who seeks only his own aggrandizement will do so in a rational, prudent, and effective way. His highest good will be his ideal of his self, and he will be willing to sacrifice much to achieve that ideal.[26]

So mental health is not equivalent to holiness. Indeed, it is those who are most open to reality who are most culpable when it comes to the decision to love their own being over the Ultimate Being. Such a preference is the essence of evil. A person can be fully aware of spiritual realities and still reject God. Such is the case with the purely spiritual beings of the fallen angels.[27]

The terse caveat that *mental health does not automatically translate into spiritual health* must here suffice, for an examination of evil is quite beyond the scope of this treatise, and indeed, of clinical psychology. The devil himself would not be a candidate for psychotherapy since he is "mentally healthy," completely in touch with reality and with the ramifications of worshipping himself rather than God.

But while mental health does not assure sanctity, sanctity's pursuit and acquisition does best assure mental health. Hence to "love the Lord thy God with thy whole heart, and with thy whole soul, and with thy whole mind, and with thy whole strength" (Mk 12:30–31) is the hallmark of existential, rational, volitional, and emotional fulfillment.

When a person transcends pride and love of self he goes beyond the conceptualization and measurement of mental health. Here, beyond psychological measurement, a person is willing to give up even his life, forfeiting the ultimate subjective good, for the sake of a higher good and truth; with the highest good and truth being God. On the natural level, this is where the magnanimous person is found, who is humble and attached to the very highest goods his unaided reason can discern. On the

---

[26] See Idealized Self-Love, 140.

[27] A certain degree of objectivity is of the essence of mortal sin: one must know that the thought, word, or act is evil (as well as freely choosing it and it being of a grave nature.)

supernatural level, here is found the saint, and sanctity is Zone Zero, the zone of infinite extension beyond.

Conclusion

The conceptualization of mental health in accord with the tripartite corresponding continuums of mental health aids the IDP clinician in properly diagnosing the level of a therapant's pathology and determining the proper method and point of intervention. For example, if a therapant presents a predominance of Zone III manifestations, he must be first engaged on the level of the visceral. For instance, the primary intervention would probably entail some form of bodily mortification that would result in the will exerting the reason's influence over the emotions of the concupiscible appetite. If a therapant presents Zone II manifestations, then he can be engaged on both the emotional and cognitive level, and challenged to turn out from his egocentric subjectivity and its ensuing distortion of reality to an objective view and valuation of himself and reality.

The Imago Dei conceptualization of tripartite corresponding continuums of mental health admits of a hierarchy in which *seeking first the kingdom of God* best assures full actualization of human potential. This demonstrates the aptness of the tripartite conceptualization of the soul, which is in harmony with the Catholic teleology of man and acknowledges sanctity as the condition that best potentiates the fathomless entirety of the human person.

CHAPTER **7**

● ● ●

IDP's Theory of Personality

A PLETHORA of personality theories abounds in clinical psychology—from Freudianism and its emphasis on libido as the catalyst of personality, to behaviorism with its emphasis on necessitated responses to external stimuli, to the latest politically correct or new age concoctions. All of these theories draw from outside of psychological science for a philosophical understanding of the nature of the person, although few acknowledge or even realize that they depend on a philosophical anthropology.

Imago Dei Psychotherapy also looks outside the science of psychology for its philosophy, but does so in an overt and systematic manner by subalternating psychological science unto a Catholic, and specifically Thomistic, understanding of the nature of the human person. Because IDP holds the premise that the Church possesses the true anthropology of the person, it confidently hypothesizes that locating the science of psychology within Catholic anthropology will bring that science to an unparalleled therapeutic efficacy.

Self, Character, and Personality

The terms *self, character,* and *personality* are understood in many different ways in both common and technical usage. Often these terms are used indiscriminately and interchangeably, but Imago Dei Psychotherapy distinguishes and defines these terms in a very specific manner. IDP categorizes the self into two distinct entities, the pseudo-self and the authentic-self.

The pseudo-self is the defensive personality and the pride and self-love at the core of that personality. The authentic-self is the imago Dei. Though all men experience the authentic-self to some degree, this experience can either be distorted and obscured by vicious character formation or defined and magnified by virtuous character formation. Together the pseudo-self and the authentic-self together with the physical body comprise the aggregate-self,[1] that is, the existing individual a man experiences upon self-reflection.

The *character* is formed by the habituation of virtue or vice. When a person engages in the moral act,[2] freely assenting to and choosing a truth and good, he impacts his character. Character is thus the result of a person either being open to and choosing the higher truths and goods that existence proffers or scorning these higher truths and goods in favor of lesser selfish pursuits. Character endures: "Sow an act, reap a habit; sow a habit, reap a character; sow a character, reap a destiny."[3] One could rightly add, "sow a destiny reap an eternity," for by habitually choosing the highest truths and goods proffered in this life, a person best assures that he will choose the highest good, which is God.

It is character's vicious elements that require the encrustation of *personality*. The personality is the result of vice's interaction with reality and thus is an apparatus of that which is vicious in the character. Personality masks the imago Dei. This is not the *persona*—social mask or image—we present to other people. Personality is rather an inner mask that a person is often

---

[1] "It is that entity, substantial, permanent, unitary, which is the subject of all the states and acts that constitute his complete life. An appeal to self-consciousness shows us that there is such a subject, of which thought, will, and feeling are modifications. It is substantial, for example, not one or all of the changing states but the reality underlying them, for our self-consciousness testifies that, besides perceiving the thought, it has immediate perception in the same act of the subject to whom the thought belongs. Just as no motion can be apprehended without some sort of apprehension of the object moved, so the perception of thought carries with it perception of the thinker. The changing states are recognized as determinations of the 'self,' and the very concept of a determination involves the presence of something determined, something not itself a determination, i.e., a substance. It is permanent, in that though one may say, 'I am completely changed,' when referring to a former state, still one knows that the 'I' in question is still the same numerically and essentially, though with certain superadded differences" (*Catholic Encyclopedia*, vol. 11, 272).

[2] See in chapter 8, "The Thomistic Moral Act."

[3] Marcus Fabius Quintilian, *De Institutione Oratoria*, I, 3, 3.

unaware of. Personality may even be fairly well hidden from others under the persona or social image, but comes out at times of high emotionality. Persona is a practical veneer that allows one to interact with people on a relatively superficial but functional level, and can be voluntarily discarded by a person or involuntarily breached by personality. Personality is not as easily discarded or breached. Personality masks others from looking in on a person's imago Dei. Personality also masks a person's own inward vision of his composite-self and his outward vision of reality.

Personality is a caricature of individuality; indeed, personalities are not unique at all. That is why psychologists can readily classify people into personality types: they have seen the personality so many times before! The person who transcends personality is he who is authentically himself; it is this person who best manifests his authentic image—the image of God in which he is made. This authentic image is a manifestation of the unfathomable, of the infinite, of the all-good that makes itself manifest in accord with the natural gifts of the person as well as in accord with his developed virtuous character.

Hence the completely virtuous man would have no "personality."[4] Contrary to what this would ordinarily connote, this does not mean he would be nondescript, but quite the contrary, for personality masks the authentic self. Without the encrustation of personality, the *imago Dei*, that which is truly unique in a person, shines forth in spontaneity and is magnified by virtue. The more virtuous a person is, the less personality is required.

Even though it is the personality that is usually equated with the unique authentic self, it is the unique, authentic self or imago Dei that is masked by a development of personality. This is the essence of the confounding paradox and supreme challenge found in the Gospels and throughout traditional Christian spirituality: *that one must die to oneself in order to live and that it is by losing one's life that one finds it.*

The Defense of Personality

An inordinate self-love and pride requires the development of personality because this self-love cannot abide by the fullness of reality, which constantly

---

[4] Before the Fall, man had no personality. Christ did not and does not have a personality, nor do the blessed in heaven, for purgation is the process of destroying self-love and pride, from whence personality derives.

militates against it. In other words, self-centeredness does not correspond to reality. Reality is painful to pride and self-love; therefore pride and self-love respond to reality by secreting the defense or filter of personality. Personality is a translation, a distortion, of reality that to some degree impedes one's full openness-to-reality. It is this preconscious/precognitive conflict between a person's pride, which places him at the center of the universe, and reality, which does not, that is the psychodynamics of personality formation.

The terms *pride* and *self-love* are used herein somewhat interchangeably, for they are part and parcel of each other. Pride entails turning away from God to turn toward self—both apostasy and selfishness. This selfishness entails the seeking of one's own temporal pleasure, which is called cupidity. All vice springs from pride and self-love or *cupidity*. St. Thomas Aquinas says:

> There are two sides to every sin, the turning toward transient satisfaction and the turning away from everlasting good. As regards the turning-toward, the principle of all sins is cupidity in its most general sense, namely, the unbridled desire for one's own pleasure. As regards the turn-ing-away, the principle is pride in its general sense, which is lack of sub-mission to God: "the beginning of pride is man's revolt from God" (Eccles 10:14). Cupidity and pride in this pervasive sense are not called capital sins, because as such they are not special sins: they are the roots and sprouts of vice, as the desire for happiness is the root of all virtue.[5]

Psychodynamically, when reality comes in contact with pride and inordinate self-love it causes the excruciating pain of negative emotions that must be alleviated or defended against. Thus, a person forms personality. Personality is a secretion of pride and self-love that protects the person from hurt. The more pride and self-love one has, the more unbearable suffering becomes. Suffering cannot be transcended because a person's love, and thus reality, does not transcend himself. When the aggrandizement of pride and the pleasure seeking of self-love are the focus of a person's desire, the suffering that comes from the buffets of reality is intolerable. All members of the fallen human race have personalities, because all men to some extent have pride and self-love.[6] The inordinateness of self-love, however, determines how pathological this personality is.

---

[5] *Quaestiones disputatae de malo,* qu. 8, art. 1, ad 1.

[6] There is a proper self-love that does not entail pride because it derives solely from loving God. This self-love is the loving of the true self for God because that self is

Thus pride and inordinate self-love make suffering, and as such reality, intolerable. As a result personality is formed to blunt that suffering and reality. Those with a pathological personality still suffer, and do so in a destructive way since they are fighting both suffering and reality. Those who are able to bypass their personality structure by transcending their self-love also suffer, but *suffer-well* and constructively. This suffering-well facilitates a person's increased openness-to-reality, whereas the pathological personality constricts and distorts a person's openness-to-reality. So too, to the extent that a person cannot suffer-well, he cannot rejoice-well, for the constriction of personality bars authentic experiencing of reality, be it negative or positive.

A person is able to enter fully into any experience if it is put into perspective. In order for a person to embrace the full spectrum of existence's sufferings and joys, he must transcend his pride and inordinate self-love.[7] The difference between suffering well and suffering poorly is the difference between *bearing* one's suffering or being *buried* by it. In the former case one embraces the suffering, allowing it to work redemptively; in the latter case one fights the suffering, which only makes it intolerable.

Uncovering the Authentic Self

In order to transcend the defenses of personality and truly become himself, a person must transcend his subjectivity by renouncing his inordinate self-love and focus on objective reality by loving things in accord with their level of being. To be self-actualized one must assent to truth: "for only through the entrance of objective reality into our being do we reach our true selfhood" (Pieper 1989, 137). Aquinas wrote, "Our intellect cannot know itself by being immediately aware of itself; but by being aware of something else it comes to itself."[8] Self-knowledge and self-actualization require that the intellect take "into itself the essential form of an objective reality" (136). *Cogito ergo sum,* then, is not a first principle, but rather *cogito,* knowing that one thinks, is dependent on objective reality impacting the intellect. As Goethe wrote: "A man knows himself only insofar as he knows the world" (137).

---

in the image of God. As the Imitation of Christ says: "He who loves God and his own soul for God despises all other love, for he sees well that God alone is eternal and incomprehensible" (Thomas á Kempis, 1976, Bk II, Sec. 5).

[7] See chapter 9.

[8] *Quaestiones disputatae de veritatem,* qu. 10, art. 8 (as cited by Pieper 1989, 137).

Self-knowledge and self-actualization, then, depend not on subjective states of mind, but on the mind's conformity to reality. Much of psychotherapy, especially the humanistic and person-centered therapies, enshrines the subjective point of view and facilitates egocentrism. Such theories increase the already inherent danger in psychotherapy to fixate on the therapant and thus produce the iatrogenic (clinically created) phenomenon of *psychovitiation*, the term introduced in IDP for psychological intervention that exacerbates or creates mental illness. This inherent danger is present even in IDP, which must utilize the subjective point of view of a therapant to remedy it effectively and is necessarily focused on the therapant in an attempt to have him confront his own egocentrism. In that psychotherapy often attempts to rectify that which did or did not take place in a therapant's upbringing, aiming at facilitating the therapant's healthy maturation, it is necessarily self-absorbing: the world, at least during therapy, once again revolves around the therapant, just as it does the child or adolescent.

But there inevitably comes a time when this subjective and egocentric stage of therapy begins to bring in diminishing returns, when the narcissism of a therapy revolving around oneself and one's thoughts and emotions is only delaying growth and becomes part of the problem. It then becomes necessary for the therapant to reorient himself from a fixation on his self to an openness-to-reality and a focus on truth. Once the therapist discerns that enough therapeutic rapport and leverage has been gained, he should begin to facilitate this reorientation by challenging the therapant's subjective egocentrism. Needless to say, an overindulgence of a therapant's egocentrism early on only makes this transition more difficult.

The crux of authentic psychotherapy is an intensely painful process, for it entails the surgical uncovering of the true self. To face one's deepest pain is to face one's authentic self. Locate the deepest pain and you locate the authentic self or imago Dei, for this pain is found beneath the encrustations of personality that seek to dull that pain and mask that imago Dei. When a person allows his personality to be breeched and suffering to bombard his self-love and pride, that self-love and pride is eroded and thus the need for personality reduced. For therapeutic efficacy a person must embrace the pain and not be determined by it. Turning from a focus on the self to objective reality, and ultimately to God and Christ Crucified, makes this suffering bearable and finally welcomed.

Suffering: The Catalyst of Human Development

In the Gospels, Our Lord admonishes his followers, "Seek ye first the Kingdom of God, and his righteousness, and all these other things shall be added unto thee" (Mt 6:33). This saying is not only mystical but practical. As practical, it accords with the understanding that transcendental values of some sort, values that go beyond the immediate objective, are advantageous to the acquiring of that goal.

The practical weighing of cost against goal often diminishes or negates the goal's value and thus reduces the drive, for the effort required and the object desired are usually somewhat equivalent. One's motivation may wane: is the goal really worth the effort? But the seeking of the final end of heaven or other transcendant values by definition have a valuation that exceeds the effort required to achieve the temporal or mundane means (i.e., proximate end). At the same time, the temporal means/proximate end derives a transcendent value by becoming a means to the transcendental end. Intense heroic effort or enduring long-suffering can be seen to be a fruit of those who hold transcendent values.

The greatest of motivational transcendent values is truth, which is, ultimately, God. This is because human person can be defined as "the one who seeks truth." But why does man seek truth? Again the catalyst is suffering. *Man seeks truth in order to alleviate or cope with suffering.*

The catalyst of suffering can be seen at the various levels of human truth seeking. For instance, on a physical level a person may seek to eradicate suffering by studying illness—immersing himself in the illness and seeking the truth about it. Moving from the *physical* level to that of the more existential, there is a *psychological* level, where a person may face and cope with the truth of the inescapability of suffering and death, for as it is said, all philosophy is a philosophy of death. And there is the *spiritual* level, where a person may seek to find meaning, indeed redemption, in suffering.

In all these "truth seeking" cases, the person is confronting, embracing, and immersing himself in reality—that is, he is disposed toward truth—and its most repellant aspect, suffering.[9] Because such a person faces reality, and does not or cannot hold as a valid option escaping suffering by denying or ignoring it, he seeks meaning in it. He seeks suffering's reason, the truth

---

[9] This disposition toward truth entails both the precognitive openness-to-reality, the cognitive sight-of-the-truth, and the volitional striving-for-the-good. See chapter 8.

about it, in hopes of alleviating it: he seeks physical cures, psychological coping, and spiritual transcendence. The reality of suffering impels him to do so.

In the seeking of truth as an antidote to suffering, suffering is embraced, studied, and at times alleviated. It is accepted for what it is. It becomes the means of growth. In that suffering is that which causes man to seek truth, we find the reason and the necessity of suffering. If suffering is embraced, if its reality is the first truth accepted, it elevates man from a mere animal existence to a seeker of truth, and, as such, ultimately a seeker of God. It is this seeking of the human heart that allows man to become more than just a creature, more than his nature: it allows him to be divinized. Suffering, then, is the catalyst for nobility, sanctity, and, ultimately, the divinization of the human being.

The will is that which opens the person up to reality and its exigencies, and hence to suffering; it is that which opens the person up to truth and makes him a *seeker of truth*. Suffering is the aspect of reality that is the essential catalyst for motivation and its engine, volition. Pleasure does not most reliably activate the will; rather, it eventually satiates it. Being driven by the mere need to escape suffering is not a free choice, but accepting suffering and either confronting it or transcending it requires free choice. Suffering is a negation, an absence of good: be it, for example, an absence of health, of life, of fulfillment, or of love. A person is able most definitively to exercise his will when he is able to choose one good to the exclusion of another good, because he would rather suffer the loss of the one over the other. Suffering that entails the loss of a good is recompensed and exceeded when the choice is made for a greater good. When a choice is made for a lesser good to the exclusion of a greater good, then the net result is an unrequited suffering. In Christian terms, this sort of suffering is the "wages of sin."

Animals will undergo suffering to avoid a greater physical suffering or because they have been conditioned to act a certain way. Only humans freely choose to suffer. Only humans more than react to actual or threatened physical pain stimuli; humans even choose to undergo suffering to alleviate existential, or nonphysical, non-immediate suffering.

Also unlike other animals that are integrally complete in their temporal existence, man is inherently incomplete; man is inherently deficient and hence fated to suffer existentially. Man is created in God's image, with free will, reason, and an immortal soul. Only God is both immortal and His own source of eternal life. Man has within him, then, the principle of eternal existence but not the source of eternal life; in short, he is a nondivine immortal being. Eternal existence without life, with life being spiritual and intellectual growth, is damnation. Man then is intrinsically needful.

Herein lies the answer to the perennial rail against God: if God is good how could He allow suffering?—because it is the only way He could divinize His creatures. God cannot make gods, because by definition God is unmade. The only way God can share His divinity with his creatures is by making a creature that can freely choose to accept his truth and his love by being open to and returning that truth and love. Without suffering, man would have no need for God. A creature that did not experience suffering would either be himself a god, which is impossible as a created being, or have its openness-to-reality constricted to the nonrational, that is, the nonhuman, level, and thus have no capacity to be divinized. But man is rational and volitional because he is made in the image of God. Because of rationality and volition, man is able to receive God's truth and love and return that truth in trusting faith and that love in disinterested adoration. This process of *fruitful receptivity* makes possible the divinization of the human creature.

Suffering will always remain to some extent a mystery in this world, for suffering's very sting is in the fact that it confounds man's intellect and repulses his will. Though suffering can be dispassionately understood as an absolute necessity for man's growth and ascendancy toward truth and God, that understanding remains wanting in the grips of an intense suffering experienced by oneself or one's loved ones; a pat understanding of suffering remains wanting because man's intellect no longer suffices in the throes of suffering. Suffering's greatest gift is procured when man is no longer able to cope with existence by means of his own resources, intellectual or otherwise, and thus he is confronted with the opportunity to reach out for God, or rather allow God to lift him up, in his vulnerability, inadequacy, and contingency. This is when man's potential for divinization is actualized by his exercise of faith. This is when man ceases to try to make himself a god and allows God to make him a son.

The Emotions

Love is the primary emotion because it is the engine of the will. Love is the emotion essential to the human act, and thus integral to the interplay between cognition and volition. When a person sees a truth cognitively he loves it; he wills it as a good he desires somehow to share in. Utilizing the Thomistic categorization, Table 7.1 delineates the essential relationship of all the emotions or passions to love. Love is the prerequisite for all the other passions. As can be seen, all the emotions have a flip side, save anger. The negative emotions are each the contrary of a positive emotion.

The emotions, or passions, are that which set the body in motion toward an end desired, hence the term "e-motion." Aquinas says that all emotions are caused by love; love is the beginning of the motion to the end loved.[10] Since all emotions stem from the emotion of love and the emotions are inordinate when there is an inordinate self-love, therefore all inordinate emotions stem from an inordinate self-love. Since love fuels the other emotions, the degree of a person's love determines the degree of the other emotions. A person then must have a great self-love or pride to have a pathological personality. A pathological personality is one that causes trouble in one's life, that manifests itself in inordinate emotions. For example, a person with serious anger problems is a person of great pride and self-love.

Love is an act of the will that is either irrational or rational. Love of self constricts reality to the realm of one's personal benefit. When one loves oneself inordinately, one cannot accept the fullness of reality, because that self-love makes the pain of existence unbearable. Developmentally a person comes to know himself, begins reflecting upon himself, only by coming into contact with an external reality.[11] All men are born with concupiscence, a darkened intellect, and a weakened will. This inherited disposition can become exacerbated by external reality, creating a self-awareness that is inordinately, and even pathologically, focused on self. This can occur for a variety of, and even paradoxical, reasons. On one hand, a child may never receive enough authentic love and affirmation from his parents and may feel acutely this deprivation. As a consequence the child must subconsciously continue to egocentrically fixate on self, that is, subconsciously increase his love of self because if he does not love himself no one else will.

---

[10] *ST* I–II, q. 26, a. 1, ad. 2.
[11] See above, "Uncovering the Authentic Self."

Table 7.1
Love-Based Emotions

Positive	Negative
Love Elicited by the good loved	*Hate* Elicited by that which destroys the good loved
Desire Elicited by a good loved not yet attained	*Repugnance* Elicited by a destructive contrary to the good loved
Delight Elicited by possessing the good loved	*Loss*[12] Elicited by not possessing the good loved
Hope Elicited by believing in the future obtainment of the good loved not yet attained	*Despair* Elicited by an unattainable good loved
Audacity/Daring Elicited by a difficult to obtain good loved	*Fear* Elicited by a danger to the good loved
Anger Elicited by harm suffered by the good loved	

Such a child lacks the parental love that allows him to turn from his infantile egocentrism. On the other hand, a child may be overly indulged, spoiled, by his parents who seek their own gratification in his reciprocal affections. As a result the child's fixation on his self as the center of the universe is reinforced.

So while the strength of the positive and negative emotions is determined by the intensity of the love present, their end determines their moral quality. IDP classifies the positive and negative emotions into *three levels of emotionality*[13] that range from the superficial and self-indulgent to the profound and sacrificial. *Pain-pleasure* is present when the end of the

---

12 "Loss" is used as opposed to the scholastic term "sorrow" so as to facilitate the differentiation of the three levels of negative emotions, which are pain, sadness, and sorrow. See in chapter 9, "The Three Levels of Emotionality."

13 The therapeutic import of the three levels of emotionality is discussed in chapter 9.

emotions is a person's own bodily sensation. *Sadness-glee* is present when the end of the emotions is a person's subjective egocentric feelings. *Sorrow-joy* is present to the degree that the end of the emotions transcends a person's subjectivity and self-interest and admits of objectivity.[14] These levels correspond respectively with the three zones of the tripartite conceptualization of mental health.

Functionality and Pathology

So, unlike mainstream psychology's characterization, it is neither functionality nor intensity of emotion that determines characterological pathology; rather it is the object of one's love that determines the morality and healthiness of that love and the other passions. An ever-waxing zeal that stems from a love of God may well be nonfunctional in the worldly sense; it may lead to persecution and even martyrdom.

The emotions in themselves are good, for they are the engines of volition. But they can be rendered bad when they are misused or misdirected. This misdirection is caused by the object of the emotion or affections. If a person has a vicious pride and inordinate love of self he will seek his own good inordinately and thus display the positive emotions in an inordinately selfish manner. As a result, he will experience the hurt of the negative emotions in an inordinate manner. Because the world does not center around any one human person and because no one person's will is law—in short, a human being is not God—these hurts of negative emotions will be unending. When love of self is the final end of a person's will, reality's rebuffs are devastatingly and unremittingly painful.

The assent to a good outside one's own subjective experience is the beginning of mental health. Emotions, then, must be tied to something outside oneself, a something that itself is not dependent on emotions—be it one's idealized future, a cause, spirituality, or the faith. Although pride and self-love are to varying degrees still elements of such an assent and love, they are nonetheless elevated from a purely visceral level to that of a rational or spiritual level.[15]

---

[14] The degree and quality of a person's sorrow-joy can range from recognizing one's objective place in the world to being open to the cosmic vicissitudes inherent in human existence.

[15] See discussion of the tripartite zones of mental health, chapter 6.

However, a person can be very functional and still suffer from inordinate self-love and pride; indeed, the most successful people can often be characterized by this. At the most grievous level, a person does not suffer from mental illness, but commits the sin of spiritual pride,[16] where he is open to spiritual reality but still prefers his own self to God. Because it in no way entails mental illness or distortions of personality, it is in no way mitigated, but rather is an outright rejection of God in preference of oneself. Such people are candidates for spiritual intervention, not psychotherapy. They are aware of their physical contingency; however, they are also aware of their spiritual immortality and would rather express a perverse will that rejects God for all eternity than submit to His omnipotence.

---

[16] Although pure spiritual pride is purportedly a rare sin, it is of the essence of all mortal sin and of damnation itself, where a person freely chooses to reject God.

CHAPTER **8**

● ● ●

IDP's Moral Agency Schema

AS FORMULATED previously, Imago Dei Psychotherapy's definition of mental health is a person's "ability to perceive, receive, reflect upon, and act upon the real." The goal of IDP goes beyond mere functionality and seeks to orient the therapant existentially, cognitively, and volitionally so as to experience an unmitigated reality and act in accord with that reality in a fully human manner. A fully human act entails the actualization of all of the elements of the above definition; indeed, their actualization is required for the performance of a moral act. For a fully human act is a moral act: one that entails choice and value, as well as a grounding in objective reality and the assumption of personal responsibility.

In order for a therapant to progress through the zones of mental health, he must increase his range and embracement of reality. To this end, this chapter introduces the Moral Agency Schema. The Moral Agency Schema is IDP's therapeutic conceptualization and provides the basic blueprint to IDP's psychotherapeutic interventive technique.

The Thomistic Moral Act

The first philosophical position considered must be epistemological or the acquirement of knowledge—"Can a person know being, and hence truth and the good?" Thomism holds an epistemology of conceptual realism,[1] where a person is able to know specific being by abstracting the essences of reality from sensation. Conceptual realism is commonsensical. It is taken for

---

[1] See chapter 4, "Conceptual Realism."

granted that one can indeed discern reality and is able to reflect validly on this reality, which is the premise for everyday activity. Man can intentionally and effectively interact with his environment because he can discern reality and truth. Conceptual realism holds that this ability is made possible by the process of abstraction. That which is abstracted is the essence of the thing perceived, not just an impression or representation.

Once it is premised that man can know being, the nature of being must be discerned. Being is the real. Although this simple definition is self-evident, the question remains: "how does the human person engage being or the real?" Being is engaged upon by man in three modes: as reality, as truth, and as the good.[2] These terms refer to the same phenomenon of being, or "that which is real." However, they are distinguished by how the human person relates to being or the real.

The first engagement, or more aptly *encounter*,[3] a person has with being is an inherent orientation or openness to it. This openness encounters the mere phenomenon of existing without cognitive consideration of specific manifestations of existence. The mere phenomenon of being without specification is often termed by Thomists as *being-as-such*; it is herein termed *reality*. This mode of encounter with the real is precognitive and experiential. It may also be termed the mode of existential encounter. Although encountering reality (being-as-such) is an inherent orientation, its full realization entails the breach of developed personality defenses that obscure reality.

Being, or the real, takes on the mode of truth when it is engaged cognitively. Aquinas states, "truth is found in all things inasmuch as they have being" (*Quaestiones disputatae de veritatem* qu. 1, art. 10). Being is in the mode of truth when considered in its potential to be known, that is, in its potential relationship to the intellect. For "truth is the proclamation of being" (Hilary, quoted in Pieper 1989, 112). In that truth emanates from

---

[2] Thomism holds that truth and the good are the essential *modes* of being in relation to a person's acquisition of being. Being, truth, and the good, along with oneness, thing (specific being), and identity, form the universal transcendentals, or that which is predicated of all that is real (*Quaestiones disputatae de veritatem* qu. 1, art. 10). However, truth and the good are those transcendentals that have a special relatedness to man, who possesses a knowing and willing mind.

[3] When referring to this precognitive, existential relation with being, the term encounter is more properly used than *engagement*, since receptivity rather than initiative procurement characterizes the role of the person in relation to being.

being and not the intellect, it requires that the intellect conform to it if the intellect is to share in it. In short, truth is objective.

Being takes on the mode of the good when it is engaged volitionally. Being is in the mode of the good when considered in its potential relation to the will, that is, in its potential to be possessed. The object of the will is always a good, that which is desirable.[4] The achieving of the good (being in relation to the will) requires the will to strive in accord with being.

These three modes of being thus form the basis for the Moral Agency Schema which is the blueprint for a therapant's engagement with the real. In the Thomistic conceptualization, reality, truth, and good find their source in the ultimate noncontingent being that is God, who is also seen as the final end of human existence.

Areas of In-Depth Psychotherapeutic Intervention

The Moral Agency Schema's use of the IDP definition of mental health as "the ability to perceive, receive, reflect upon, and act upon the real" entails existential, cognitive, and volitional elements. For therapeutic purposes and in accord with a Thomistic model, the existential dynamic is viewed as a person's *openness-to-reality*, the cognitive dynamic as the *sight-of-the-truth*,[5] and the volitional dynamic as *striving-for-the-good*. Openness-to-reality is the prerequisite disposition of receptivity that a person must have in order to gain an unhampered sight-of-the-truth. The intellect's sight-of-the-truth then presents that truth to the will as a good to be attained, thus bringing into play striving-for-the-good. Again, when being is the subject of precognitive encounter it is termed *reality*, when the subject of intellect it is termed *truth*, and when the subject of the will it is termed *good*.

Openness-to-reality is the deepest level of the therapeutic intervention. It is the prerequisite existential disposition where the consciousness of the therapant is opened up to *being-as-such*. Being-as-such is being in itself, in a nonparticularized form. Being-as-such could be described as *existence as a transcendental*. Being-as-such is encountered precognitively, for cognition

---

4 The good desired, however, may not be the highest good presented at the time and by its choice may even destroy a higher good.

5 In the interests of simplicity, what Aquinas refers to as sight of the good is here referred to as sight-of-the-truth. Although the intellect presents the being to the will as good, it still, strictly speaking, encounters that being as truth.

requires a particularization of being. This precognitive encounter is due to the mind's being made for or preprogrammed for encountering being.

Once openness-to-reality is present, reality's particularizations, its manifestations in things, can be cognitively engaged and thus become truth. This cognitive engagement takes place in the second area of therapeutic intervention, sight-of-the-truth. Intervention in the area of sight-of-the-truth is the cognitive piece of the therapeutic process and works to facilitate the therapant's understanding of reality as truth.

Once the sight-of-the-truth is acquired, the therapant has an end in sight that can be striven for as a good. Sight-of-the-truth eventually leads to the third area of the therapeutic intervention, striving-for-the-good, where the will desires and intends to achieve the good.

When the sight-of-the-truth is coupled with striving-for-the-good an act becomes fully moral or human: "Those acts are called human of which a man is master, and he is master of actions in virtue of his reason and will" (*ST* I–II, q. 1, a. 1).

In accord with a Thomistic understanding of the moral act, there are various partial steps that finally unite sight-of-the-truth and striving-for-the-good, which again is the culmination of the fully moral/human act.[6] Each step involves the intellective faculty extending itself into the volitional faculty, thus uniting reason and will. These Thomistic steps form the basis of the Moral Agency Schema that pinpoints and defines the critical therapeutic areas of Imago Dei psychotherapeutic intervention as diagramed in Figure 8.1. Note well that the actual dynamics of the moral act are much more complex than depicted in the step-by-step schema. For instance, because each step requires some element of judging the good, both primordial conscience and judgment are involved to some degree in each step. The schema provides an accurate, even if necessarily inadequate, representation of the Thomistic moral act. For clinical purposes, it provides a highly efficacious framework for psychotherapy.

Moral Agency Schema

The left side of the Moral Agency Schema shows the succession of the cognitive partial acts, and the right side the succession of the volitional partial

---

6 These steps were not definitively outlined by Aquinas, but have been derived and compiled by Thomists from his various works.

Figure 8.1
The Imago Dei Moral Agency Schema[7]

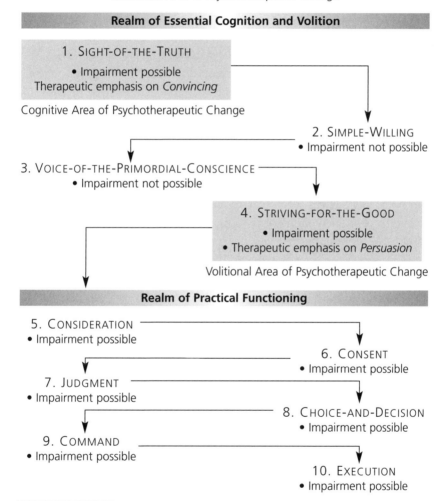

Realm of the Preconscious

OPENNESS-TO-REALITY
- Impairment possible
- Therapeutic emphasis on *Encountering*

Existential Area of Psychotherapeutic Change

Realm of Essential Cognition and Volition

1. SIGHT-OF-THE-TRUTH
- Impairment possible
Therapeutic emphasis on *Convincing*

Cognitive Area of Psychotherapeutic Change

2. SIMPLE-WILLING
- Impairment not possible

3. VOICE-OF-THE-PRIMORDIAL-CONSCIENCE
- Impairment not possible

4. STRIVING-FOR-THE-GOOD
- Impairment possible
- Therapeutic emphasis on *Persuasion*

Volitional Area of Psychotherapeutic Change

Realm of Practical Functioning

5. CONSIDERATION
- Impairment possible

6. CONSENT
- Impairment possible

7. JUDGMENT
- Impairment possible

8. CHOICE-AND-DECISION
- Impairment possible

9. COMMAND
- Impairment possible

10. EXECUTION
- Impairment possible

---

[7] The skeletal configuration of Figure 8.1 is based on the *Thomistic Structure of Moral Acts* (Pieper, 1989), 179.

acts, which together lead up to the execution of a fully moral/human act. Three areas—openness-to-reality (which has been added as a prerequisite step to the subsequent steps of the Thomistic moral act), sight-of-the-truth, and striving-for-the-good—are areas of intense, in-depth psychotherapy. The prerequisite step, openness-to-reality, is the area of existential intervention; the first step, sight-of-the-truth, is the area of cognitive intervention; and the fourth step, the striving-for-the-good, is the area of volitional intervention. Aquinas holds that steps 2 and 3, simple-willing and the voice-of-the-primordial-conscience *(synderesis)*, are essentially automatic, determined processes. These two areas are not directly subject to psychological impairment and are therefore not areas of therapeutic intervention.

In addition to the enumeration of steps, the entire Moral Agency Schema is divided into three sections to denote the nature of the possible psychological impairment.[8] The first section consists only of openness-to-reality, and is the existential *realm of the subconscious.* The second section, which consists of steps 1 through 4, is the *realm of essential cognition and volition.* It is in these first two realms that the intense psychotherapeutic dynamics takes place. The third section of the schema is the *realm of practical functioning.* This realm, which consists of steps 5 through 10, deals with counseling or the practical dynamics of implementing and becoming habituated to striving-for-the-good, and diminishing that which impedes this striving; it deals with the establishment of virtue and disestablishment of vice.

Openness-to-Reality

Aquinas demarcates the various levels of openness-to-reality that are possible for the human person: "The entire range . . . can be ordered into three levels. One . . . concerns only the body. . . . Then there is the . . . power that relates to a wider sphere; namely, to all material objects accessible through the senses. . . . A third kind . . . is directed toward an even more comprehensive sphere of objects: not only toward all material things, but toward all that exists" (*ST* I, q. 78).

---

[8] Although the voice of primordial conscience (synderesis) begins to extend the intellect toward the practical action of seeking the good, it is more ordered toward the theoretical realm of ideal and aspiration toward a goal than it is toward the practical realm of implementation and means toward a goal. Thus, for therapeutic purposes, the voice of primordial conscience is categorized as an essential psychological process.

Openness-to-reality is to sight-of-the-truth as opening the eyes is to vision. Openness-to-reality is thus the prerequisite existential disposition that is required if one is to gain an integral sight-of-the-truth. In this pre-cognitive, prevolitional realm of the subconscious, the therapeutic empha-sis is on *encountering*. Openness-to-reality requires a positive dispositional openness to or encountering of reality that is ever waxing. Thomism holds that "the spirit-based self, ordered as it is toward the whole of reality, is in its very essence called to face with an attitude of receptive, unbiased open-ness this universality of its world" (Pieper 1989, 98). Because reality itself is limitless, a person's openness-to-reality requires this positive dynamic of openness; stagnation does not suffice. Such an openness requires the courageous overcoming of fears and the subsequent personality defenses that shelter one from transcendent being and the ultimate concerns that come with realizing the contingency of one's own particular being.

To be dynamically open to reality occurs in a precognitive-prevolitional realm, for it entails the encounter with being-as-such. Openness-to-reality takes place on the precognitive or subconscious level because "a mutual correlation between being and mind exists already prior to any actual per-ception [or] activity of the mind" (Pieper 1989, 62). It is important to note that reality emanates from the object known, not the knowing mind. "Reality in itself is oriented toward man's perceiving mind, without the mind's contribution, and simply by virtue of its very *being*, which man has not bestowed upon it." As such, reality and subsequently truth, is objec-tive as opposed to subjective.

The encounter with being-as-such allows one a perspective in which to view particular beings, oneself especially, as contingent manifestations of being-as-such. From such an existential platform, a person is now in place to engage cognitively a particular being objectively.[9] This objective perspec-tive is essential to mental health, allowing a person to stand outside his sub-jective self, that is, pseudo-self, and so evaluate his emotions, cognitions, and actions, stepping outside the vicious circle of such impairments as neu-rotic anxiety, negative cognitions, obsessive compulsive actions, or psy-chotic fixations.

Therapeutic interventions on the level of openness-to-reality aim at facil-itating a therapant's encountering of reality. Here techniques of existential

[9] This is done in Step 3 of the moral act, sight-of-the-truth.

psychotherapy are to be employed. Central to such techniques is the induce-
ment of *borderline experiences*, that is, inducing encounters with the ultimate
concerns of human existence, namely isolation, the search for meaning, freedom, and death (Yalom 1980). These existential concerns must be embraced
fully in their painful reality. But to do so, a therapant must be able to breech
and reduce his personality defenses and even the aversion to truth that stems
from original sin, allowing the pain to pass through his pride and self-love to
his deepest self, to his imago Dei. In doing so the pride and self is devastated
to some degree, which in turn reduces the vigor and need for the defenses
that the pride and self-love secrete to insulate itself from the pain of reality
and accordingly allow a therapant a fuller openness-to-reality. (see chapter 9,
Mechanisms of Psychotherapy)

Finally, it is in the Realm of the Preconscious that the therapant is
encountered *Dasein*-in-Christ. This is an encounter of the therapant in his
being-as-such, as in his being in the image of God, and in his being in
potential as a sanctified son of God. This encounter must remain the essential relationship throughout the therapeutic process. Indeed, this encounter
remains the basis for effective work in both the Realms of Cognition and
Volition. (See *Dasein*-in-Christ chapter 10, pg. 159)

Sight-of-the-Truth

To the degree that a person is existentially open to reality he is able to view the
truth. Again, the truth is the cognition of that which exists: it is being proclaimed. Thus, in order to gain sight-of-the-truth a person must have the
proper disposition; a person must be open to reality. When openness-to-reality
is of the spiritual or transcendent depth, Aquinas's third level of awareness, the
sight-of-the-truth, transcends subjectivism. However, this subordination of
subjectivity to objectivity does not automatically entail full sight-of-the-truth.
Once a person's openness-to-reality and objectivity is established, the truth
must be brought into sight so that it can be assented to.

A person may be *unaware* of all the truth that is seeable, or may be *closed-
off* to some of that truth in an inordinate focus upon particular truths. Being
unaware of the truth is a result of ignorance. Ignorance is rectified at the stage
of sight-of-the-truth through therapeutic pedagogy. The therapeutic intervention required so to rectify ignorance of the truth is *convincing*.

Convincing is an intellectual process that entails a pedagogy of the truth. When a therapant is sufficiently open to reality, identification of truth and the subsequent convincing of the truth may take place. An essential part of this pedagogy entails equating truth with the good, thus facilitating the next therapeutic step of striving-for-the-good.

Convincing, or the pedagogy of truth, should be as Socratic in method as possible; it should allow the therapant to discover the truth. This Socratic method of facilitated self-discovery should be implemented to the full extent that the therapant's mental state allows. Of course, encounter's increase of existential awareness and convincing's pedagogy of truth do not take place only once, but rather it is a gradual spiraling process that continually recycles to effect the therapant's ever-deepening openness-to-reality and sight-of-the-truth.

Psychotherapeutic techniques of convincing employed at the level of sight-of-the-truth are cognitive in nature. Thus techniques of cognitive psychotherapy can be employed. For example, helping a therapant identify and rectify false, fallacious, or inconsistent thinking is integral to gaining sight-of-the-truth. However, while some cognitive techniques may tend toward producing positive or optimistic thought patterns, intervention in accord with the Moral Agency Schema seeks to foster realistic thought patterns. Intervention in any of the three areas of psychotherapeutic change seeks to rectify thoughts so that they correspond with objective reality, regardless of the subjective impact, be it negative or positive, that this assent to reality has on the temporal comfort of the person. It is the recognition of uncomfortable truths that is the catalyst of therapeutic change.

Vice, Vice-Effect, and Inherited Concupiscence

Whereas being unaware of the truth is the result of ignorance, *being closed-off to truth* is the result of vice. Vice is here defined as habitually focusing on lower truths and choosing lower goods to the detriment of more profound truth or higher goods. Although being closed-off to truth has its specific result in the second area of therapeutic change, sight-of-the-truth, its cause, vice, impacts all facets of the person. Thus intervention in regard to being closed-off involves all three areas of therapeutic change, that is, both openness-to-reality's existential encountering, sight-of-the-truth's cognitive convincing, and striving-for-the-good's volitional persuasion, as well as the realm of practical functioning.

A person's impaired sight-of-the-truth is rarely a result only of ignorance, but entails vice as well. Ignorance facilitates vice, and vice facilitates ignorance. Vice is the result of disordered choices that are volitional and habitual. But not all people affected by vice are responsible for the vice, for some may have their sight-of-the-truth impaired by being exposed to the vice of others. This occurs when reason is debilitated and exposure occurs. This *vice-effect's* gravest harm is often found in those victims of childhood abuse or neglect who have internalized the evil, an internalization that may have occurred even before they have reached the age of reason. Victims of overwhelming trauma may also "lose" their reason during the trauma. In both cases, a person has formed an association of a particular stimulus with a particular end via the memory. This is similar to the way animals learn. It is an unreasoned reaction to a stimulus. Thus those suffering under vice-effect are not engaging in a moral act and hence cannot form habits, that is, vices or virtues, in regard to that vice-effect. The presence of vice-effect in a victim, unlike the presence of vice in a perpetrator, does not denote personal culpability.

Vice-effect does, however, create a disposition that can sway a person toward making vicious choices himself. This is similar to the natural disposition toward vice that Aquinas calls an *inherited concupiscence* (*ST* I–II, q. 82, a. 1). In the Catholic tradition, Aquinas attributes this concupiscence to original sin; however, the tendency to seek "creature comforts" over arduous endeavors, pleasure over pain, is a principle that even a strict material behaviorism depends upon in its therapeutic conceptualization. Note well that vice, vice-effect, and inherited concupiscence all have their origins in evil, be it respectively, a person's own sin, the exposure to the sins of others, or inherited original sin.

In any case, whether a therapant is subject to a blinding vice voluntarily or to involuntary vice-effect and inherited concupiscence (and it is usually a combination of various proportions), it is the end of therapy to repair the sight-of-the-truth and subsequently restore the freedom to choose the truth as the good. As such, and even if the process is preceded by a gentle remedying of the past traumas of an innocent victim, a therapant is finally asked to take moral responsibility for his actions and life.

The need ever to increase openness-to-reality and hone the sight-of-the-truth is the need for a person to grow constantly by dying to falsehood and assenting to truth. The habitual disposition to do so is the true mark of mental health.

Striving-for-the-Good

The next two steps of the Imago Dei Moral Agency Schema, simple-willing and voice-of-the-primordial-conscience, are not areas of therapeutic intervention since they are not subject to impairment. The second step, simple-willing, cannot be impaired because of the unavoidable attraction and love of a good once it is sighted. The third step, voice-of-the-primordial-conscience *(synderesis)*, cannot be impaired because this voice is always imperative, always demands that good be done and evil avoided. However, if the sight-of-the-truth is impaired—either viciously or organically—a detrimental good whose attainment destroys a greater good may present itself to these processes to the exclusion of that greater good.

It is in the fourth step, that of striving-for-the-good, that is found the second of the two areas of intervention that are possible in the realm of essential cognition and volition. In that both sight-of-the-truth and striving-for-the-good are the only two areas of intervention located within this realm, they are, as such, the only areas in which intense or in-depth psychotherapy takes place. Whereas the prerequisite step of openness-to-reality is the existential area of psychotherapeutic intervention and the first step (sight-of-the-truth) is the cognitive area of intervention, the fourth step (striving-for-the-good) is the volitional area of psychotherapeutic intervention.

In the volitional realm of striving-for-the-good the therapant must exert the effort to achieve the good by exercising and strengthening his will. Whereas intervention in the area of openness-to-reality entails a therapant's *encountering* the truth of being and sight-of-the-truth entails *convincing* a therapant of that truth, intervention in the area of striving-for-the-good requires *persuading* the therapant of the necessity of acquiring that truth as a good.

Striving-for-the-good can be impaired when the will refuses to heed the imperative command of the intellect's voice of primordial conscience. If this is the case, the therapeutic dynamics of *persuasion* is required. A therapist must facilitate a therapant's heeding of the imperative command to will the good in its entirety, not just a truncated version of it. The therapant must find the inspiration to will the entire good by striving for the highest good he perceives. However, to rouse a therapant out of an indifference to the imperative commands of good, truth, and reality is often very difficult. Much of the art of psychotherapy consists of this ability to persuade a therapant to awaken from an existential somnolence and a hedonistic ethos. The therapist must be able to locate and prudently "push the buttons" of a therapant that will awaken a sense of urgency and a disgust with enslavement to bodily sensation and emotions, and thus activate the will. Again, Imago Dei Psychotherapy holds that these metaphorical buttons may be located in different areas of a person's psyche and manifest under a sundry of symptoms, but are all eventually wired to root existential concerns.

Therapeutic persuasion entails finding within a therapant the motivational keys that will trigger a sense of urgency. The circular dynamics of the Moral Agency Schema can be seen in the Imago Dei Psychotherapy holding that the motivational keys are at root deemed to be existential concerns, such as death and meaninglessness, that need to be progressively unmasked. This in effect brings the therapeutic process back to the beginning existential area of openness-to-reality.

Intervention in the Moral Agency Schema's realm of psychotherapeutic intervention, then, requires that the psychotherapist effectively challenge the therapant to become discontented with himself, indeed, to do violence to himself because he is not living up to his human vocation as a "seeker of truth." The Basque poet-philosopher Miguel de Unamuno (1905) wrote:

> There are small minds who assert that it is better to be a contented pig than an unhappy human being. But he who has once tasted the flavor of humanity, he will—even in profound misery—prefer the unhappiness of man to the contentment of the pig. It is well, therefore to cause disquietude in human souls and to enkindle in them a mighty yearning. (159)[10]

Facilitating such a "disquietude" and "mighty yearning," or striving-for-the-good, is essential to any real and deep psychotherapeutic change. It is also essential both to growth as a person and ultimately, in the Thomistic scheme of things, to sanctification.

---

[10] Alternative translation of Reinhardt (1952, 234).

Striving's Mortification of the Intellect

Josef Pieper (1989) refers very briefly in his works to an *asceticism of knowledge* that is required of a person in his pursuit and perception of objective reality: "A tremendous activity of the will is required if we are to be determined only by reality in our knowing, to be objective and to force ourselves to silence and keep ourselves out of the picture and so become perceptive" (135).

An ever-waxing openness-to-reality and sight-of-the-truth then requires not only a striving of the will toward the good, but also a concomitant and continual dying to oneself. Specifically, openness-to-reality and sight-of-the-truth requires mortification of the intellect. This mortification requires that a person always assent to the full hierarchy of goods that is present in objective reality. It also entails mortifying the imagination and memory so that these intellectual powers do not obstruct, but rather facilitate, that assent. Mortification is an act of the will, therefore these powers of the intellect are mortified by the will. Specifically, when in striving-for-the-good the will accepts the intellect's presentation of a good, it also accepts the mortification required to attain that good. Mortification is present whenever a lower good is sacrificed for a higher good.

The sight-of-the-truth and striving-for-the-good work together synergistically. A person sees the good only dimly or indefinitely at first, but nonetheless desires it. The primordial conscience then affirms with certitude that it is a good to be sought or one to be avoided because it destroys a greater good, which is followed by choosing to strive to attain the good proffered or choosing to reject the acquirement of good because of its destruction of a higher good. Whether or not this striving-for-the-good is in accord with the voice of primordial conscience, which conveys objective truth and its hierarchy of goods, dictates whether the choice redounds upon the intellect's sight-of-the-truth to its improvement or to its impairment. If the focus of striving-for-the-good is ordinate, either it does no harm to the sight-of-the-truth or it increases this sight's acuity. If striving-for-the-good's focus is inordinate, it can cause the sight-of-the-truth to become myopic.

A person chooses a lower good over a higher good because his emotions bind his reason. These binding emotions stem from self-love and pride. A guilty conscience will subsequently threaten this self-love and pride which will erect subconscious defenses against this threat and other threatening realities that still cause pain even though one has chosen to exclude them from consciousness. This is why sacrificing lower goods desired by pride and self-love for higher goods demanded by love of God does violence to and diminishes that pride and self-love and allows a therapant to advance into or in Zone I of mental health and beyond.

Ordinate or inordinate striving-for-the-good also strengthens or habituates the will itself for good or ill, either rectifying or exacerbating its disorder. The darkening of the intellect by either original sin or actual sin is called ignorance. The disordering of the will by either original or actual sin is called malice. In moral terms, temptation occurs in the sight-of-the-truth and sin occurs in the striving. Thus moral culpability takes place in the realm of volitional striving, and sin incurs when the will strives toward a lower good to the detriment of a higher good. Evil itself can be defined as the willing of a lower good at the expense of a higher one. Eventually, the sight-of-the-truth can become blinded to reality by the will's continually ignoring the objective hierarchy of goods in favor of a subjective focusing on a lower good severed from the rest of reality.

Man's free will and his destiny to love God (and hence be divinized) requires that his sight-of-the-truth not be completely impelling, for if sight-of-the-truth impelled a person to love ordinately, this love could not be true love, for it would not entail free choice. So too, because of the intellect's dimming and suffering from ignorance because of sin, its sight-of-the-truth is made still less acute. Asceticism of knowledge, where there must be a volitional striving to focus on objective truth and a doing of violence to subjective distortions, then, is required of all men.

If even the great clear-sightedness of the angels did not prevent a third of them from falling from heaven, how can man, whose intellect is inferior to that of the angels, trust an untrained and unmortified intellect to ascertain the good? To assent to the objective truth, the hierarchy of goods, requires not only volitional effort, but mortification—a violence to one's pride and self-love and one's subsequent subjective distortions—because the choice of a higher good often entails the sacrifice of a desired lower one. For those who suffer neurosis and psychosis, this asceticism of knowledge requires a specific mortification of the imagination and memory. For imagination and memory in the service of a radical subjectivism always results in a distortion of reality and may result in delusions or hallucinations.

Hierarchy of Goods

Effective therapeutic intervention in the areas of moral agency requires the use of Aristotelian hierarchy of goods that was adopted by St. Thomas Aquinas. Specifically, a person closes himself off to aspects of reality by the rejection of higher goods or by fixation on lower goods that exclude higher goods. Higher goods may threaten the free acquisition of certain lower goods and therefore be rejected in favor of those lower goods. For example, the good of carnal pleasure sought via promiscuity can destroy the higher good of chastity or marital love. The passions can indeed blind a person. When a person strives for or focuses on the incomplete or inordinate good, it affects his field of vision and he becomes characterologically myopic because he must turn away from, block out, or defend against the greater reality that threatens the pride and self-love he serves. When this turning away from reality becomes predominate it is then manifestly pathological, and a person is in Zone II or III of mental health.

Thus, a person can reject the good in view, or focus on a lesser aspect of it. If done habitually, a person's willful rejection of the good will cause impairment to his sight-of-the-truth and close off his openness-to-reality. In the vicious character, the destruction of the higher good becomes concomitant with the attainment of the lower good, and thus evil is fused with a lower good.

Whereas focusing on a lower good can impair the sight of a higher good and necessarily repudiates that good as higher, focusing on a higher good never destroys sight of a lower good. Rather, the focusing on the higher good defines the lower good in the light of proper context. Even the exclusion of a lower good in favor of a higher good, such as when a person chooses evangelical celibacy over marriage, does not repudiate that lower good but only recognizes it as lower. Although various religious sects and heresies may not recognize or incorporate lower goods into their worldview, the orthodox Catholic position as an incarnational, cultural, and sacramental worldview celebrates these lower goods and actually raises them up because they are ultimately ordered toward the highest good.

The hierarchy of goods espoused by IDP is that of classical philosophy as opposed to the type popularized by such as Maslow. It has nothing to do with one's subjective needs, but rather with objective reality. While

134 • IMAGO DEI PSYCHOTHERAPY

both promise self-actualization as an end goal, it is only the classic para-digm that can deliver this self-actualization. What are valid in Maslow's hierarchy of needs are the self-evident exigencies entailed in mortal exis-tence. Even when struggling for his very life, a man is no less human and need not be any less open to the totality of reality than he would be in a pristine contemplative setting. Indeed, some would argue that in the face of death many men are the most open to reality, for objective truth gains entrance through the coercive reality of death. As it is said, "There are no atheists in foxholes."

Realm of Practical Functioning

Although it is in the upper realm of essential openness, cognition, and volition that in-depth psychotherapy takes place, intervention in the lower realm of practical functioning is a necessary augmentation to these essen-tial areas of psychotherapeutic intervention, and as such is an essential part of Imago Dei Psychotherapy. It is in the realm of practical functioning that the human act is consummated and habituated. This is the realm of the virtues and, as such, an essential part of a therapeutic process based on a Thomistic conceptualization. Behavioral techniques are especially appli-cable to intervention at this stage.

The steps of the realm of practical function, like those of essential cogni-tion and volition, also alternate between acts of the intellect and acts of the will. These steps are consideration (cognitive), consent (volitional), judgment (cognitive), choice-and-decision (volitional), command (cognitive), and exe-cution (volitional).

If a person does not need in-depth therapy but rather counseling in living and functioning, it is the practical psychological processes that are dealt with. However, impairment in the essential psychological processes, in the areas of sight-of-the-truth and striving, always manifests itself in the practical psycho-logical processes, since these latter processes are dependent on the former. Behavioral techniques are employed in this realm to augment and bring to fruition the cognitive and existential techniques involved in the essential areas of psychotherapeutic intervention, for not only does how a person thinks affect how he acts, but how a person acts affects how he thinks.

While a thorough consideration of the theoretical nature and therapeu-tic implications of the virtues as they apply to counseling in the realm of practical functioning is outside the scope of this treatise, the following is offered as an indication of their therapeutic importance and their irreplaceable inclusion in Imago Dei Psychotherapy.

To implement volition in accord with the good requires the cardinal virtues: prudence, fortitude, temperance, and justice. Prudence is that which guides a person's judgment, and is the prerequisite for the other cardinal virtues. Justice is that which guides a person's interpersonal actions and familial and social obligations. Hence, justice is a crucial factor in the myriad of interpersonal problems that plague the psychologically impaired. It is also the objective standard of action that is mandated regardless of one's personal loss or gain: justice is the objective limiter of subjective self-interest. Fortitude is that which enables the person to overcome obstacles and face adversity and fear. A therapant can have clear sight-of-the-truth and strive strongly toward it as the good, but if he lacks fortitude he will not be able to undergo the crucible of concretizing his choice for the good. This choice of the good always entails the mortification of a lesser good, which has held the therapant in its throes. Temperance is that which enables a person to delay gratification or forgo lesser goods for the sake of higher goods. The ability to delay gratification is essential to the accomplishment of any arduous endeavor, psychotherapy included, and is often quite debilitated in the psychologically impaired. These moral or cardinal (in Latin *cardo*, which means hinge) virtues all interact with each other. For instance, it takes fortitude to be temperate, and temperance is a necessary element of fortitude, while fortitude is often required to act justly, and prudence is required to discern the just action.

It is most appropriate that a Catholic clinical psychology have this emphasis on virtue, rather than vice, for it rests on the teleological principles of sanctification and perfection and offers the supernatural channels of sacramental grace to achieve this end. Thus IDP focuses not on abnormality, but rather on potentiality. Diagnosis of vice is necessary to ascertain how in virtue one must progress, but it is the establishment of the virtue that best eradicates the vice.

● ● ●

CHAPTER 9

IDP's Mechanisms
of Psychotherapy

IMAGO DEI Psychotherapy holds personality to be the defensive secretion of a person's inordinate pride and self-love against the pain of reality. The therapeutic process essentially entails the breaching of these personality defenses so that pride and self-love can be diminished. When this occurs, the therapant begins to free his reason and will from the bondage of his emotions. He becomes more cognizant of truth and able to choose it as the good, and he is more open to reality.

The foundational truth to be cognizant of is that one's pride and self-love is indeed inordinate and that one is not the center of the universe but rather a contingent, vulnerable, and even wretched creature. If volitionally accepted, this truth is deadly to that pride and self-love. The corollary to this truth about oneself is that there is something else that must be the center of the universe, omnipotent, and perfect.[1]

Assenting to objective truth and submitting to the subsequent pain begins to dissolve the inordinate pride and self-love of the therapant, progressively reducing the need for the defenses of personality. The more the therapeutic process permeates personality and works caustically on self-love and pride, the more successful the psychotherapy. In-depth psychotherapy is an excruciating process: there is no such thing as a painless psychotherapy that is effective.

---

[1] It is in the adoration of God that a person properly derives his own self-worth and rightly ordered self-love. Rightly ordered love of self is loving oneself in God, for God, and because of God; thus it is truly a love of God.

The therapant must undergo suffering and learn to suffer-well if he is to progress in therapy. To suffer-well a person must transcend himself, that is, his own self-love, so that he may bear rather than be buried by his suffering. While a person's self-love and pride makes suffering overwhelming or too much to handle, a person who is able to transcend his self-love is also able to embrace fully his suffering because his self-love and concomitant personal suffering is not the all-encompassing focal point of his existence.

Being open to suffering is being open to reality, inclusive of the joys of life. Breaching the personality defenses against suffering allows a person to live the fullness of the human experience, both its sorrows and its joys. To suffer-well, then, is a catalyst to growth, to a fuller openness to and love of reality, and to an authentic human existence; it is the catalyst of mental health.

The Three Levels of Emotionality

The therapeutic process of suffering-well entails an ascent through three levels of emotions:[2] the visceral, the binding, and the marshaled. Visceral emotionality is on the level of *pain-pleasure*, binding emotionality is on the level of *sadness-glee*, and marshaled emotionality is on the level of *sorrow-joy*. These levels of emotionality range from the superficial to the profound and correspond to the three zones of mental health,[3] and entailing an increasing openness-to-reality.[4] Like the three zones of mental health, the three levels of emotionality are not exclusive of one another, but refer rather to that emotionality that is dominant.

In the IDP process therapants are systematically challenged to identify, embrace, and transcend their deepest suffering,[5] which is done by therapeutically leading them through the three levels of suffering. If a therapant is experiencing the domination of visceral emotions he must be brought to the realization that physical feelings of pain do not touch upon who he essentially is as a person. If a therapant is experiencing the domination of binding emotions he must come to view his degree of sadness as indicative of his degree of self-love. In both cases the process entails moving from a purely

[2] Emotions are either positive or negative, and all stem from the emotion of love. See in chapter 7, Table 7.1. Love-Based Emotions.

[3] See in chapter 6, "Emotion."

[4] See in chapter 8, "Openness-to-Reality."

[5] People who are experiencing a surfeit of pleasure do not seek psychotherapy; it is only when they experience the other side of the coin, suffering, that they seek alleviation.

subjective encounter with suffering to a more objective encounter. When this is done a therapant is positioned to move into the realm of sorrow, which entails, to varying degrees, an objective encounter with the suffering inherent in human existence and its particular manifestation in the therapant's life.

When in the throes of grave mental illness, many therapants experience the complete domination of visceral emotions. A person who is fixated on his physical feelings to the point of being irrational (Zone III) will have negative emotions ordered to (real or imagined) physical *pain* and positive emotions ordered to (real or imagined) physical *pleasure*. A person who is so dominated by his visceral emotions has his reality constricted down to physical sensation.

A person who primarily experiences binding emotions is fixated on his own physical and psychological feelings (Zone II). He is reasonable to an extent, for his reason is bound by his emotions and self-love and pride, and thus in the service of emotions. Reason when so bound by the emotions is ultimately subjective and thus distorts reality. A person who is experiencing binding emotions will have negative emotions that are characterized by sadness. In IDP terminology, sadness is a subjective self-pity, when it is all-consuming it is psychological depression. Such a person will have positive emotions that are characterized by glee, which is a subjective feeling of being pleased or experiencing satisfied gratification, when it is all-consuming it is psychological mania. Both sadness and glee and the events that cause them are distorted and magnified to the extent that a person has self-love and pride: *if a person feels he is the very center of the universe, all that affects him, for good or ill, is cataclysmic.*

A person who primarily experiences marshaled emotions has either idealized his self-love (see next section) or died to it and will predominately experience negative emotions of *sorrow* and positive emotions of *joy*. Sorrow and joy are emotions that to a greater or lesser extent derive from an objective view of the vicissitudes of life. A person will have peace of soul to the degree he is able to accept the full objective spectrum of sorrows and joys that life entails. Of course, such an objectivity clearly and proportionally locates one's own sufferings within the universal spectrum of human suffering and thus requires that one correctly locate himself within the order of existence as a contingent creature among the countless multitudes.

These three classifications refer both to the emotionality that is presently dominant for a person and to the emotionality that is habitually experienced. As such, a person who is habituated to one emotionality still experiences the other two in a subordinate degree. So too, under various circumstances any one of the three emotionalities may become *temporarily* dominant. This can happen, for instance, to a person habituated to marshaled emotions who is confronted with great physical pain and thus reacts by focusing on the preservation of his bodily good, which is a necessary response. It may also happen on the other end of the spectrum, where a person habituated to visceral emotions temporarily focuses on other people's suffering, thereby assenting to an objective perception of suffering that is characteristic of the marshaled emotions. A person truly ensconced in marshaled emotionality would give his life if objectivity demanded it and would never take his life though his visceral emotions demanded it. On the other hand, a person habituated to visceral emotions will quickly revert to a fixation on his own bodily concerns once the distracting stimuli of another's suffering diminishes.

Idealized Self-Love

In idealized self-love, a person objectifies his own ideal of self. He objectively evaluates where his actual state at present falls short from this ideal and embraces the sorrow that emanates from this discrepancy, spurring him on to taking whatever steps are necessary to remediate this discrepancy. His joy derives from the achievement of the ideal and even from the ideal itself. To achieve the ideal self and requite the idealized self-love, a person must delay gratification and deny himself. Thus achieving the ideal self entails doing violence to some aspect of the pseudo-self.

As long as a person is achieving his idealized self, satisfying his idealized self-love, he will achieve a certain equilibrium—if not actual peace—of soul. Once this achievement wanes or once he has accomplished all he set out to do, or if he fails, he will feel the pain of an unrequited self-love. At such a time, he has two choices. First, he can find a new cause to live for, either a new idealized self or a cause outside his own self-love. To champion a cause outside oneself is to reorient from the self to some extent, and thus it means further to embrace objective reality.

A person may also fall back into a subjective self-love of binding emotions when he finds the idealized future or self to be wanting or experiences failure. Here he can rest on his laurels (which is not living in the moment, is a form of stagnation, and is conducive to ennui) or he may seek in some other ways to feed his self-love and pride and anesthetize his pain.

It is not only successful men but all men of character who to some extent idealize their self-love, future, and selves. This is equally true of those who embrace religion. Thus, for the religious person spiritual pride is the great occupational hazard and the last hurdle to overcome before he becomes not only religious but holy. However, when a person's worldview and idealization of self entails the recognition of a person's creaturehood in relationship to God Omnipotent, as well as the ideals of self-abnegation and humiliation, dying to oneself and the purgation of spiritual pride is at least cognitively assented to, which facilitates its volitional actuality. When a person becomes habituated to dying to himself through the practice of religion and the acceptance of the humiliations, he is poised on the threshold of sanctity. A final remedy that God may graciously visits upon his elect is a dark night of the soul, which, if embraced, causes a person to die completely to himself and to love God completely for His own sake.

Realm of Marshaled Emotions

Like Zone I of mental health, marshaled emotions admit of both those who are still motivated by self-love and pride but who have idealized this self-love and pride and those who are dying to this self-love and pride. The driven and highly successful businessman or athlete typifies the person who falls into the fall first category; the saint typifies those who fall into the second.

Most contemporary psychotherapies prescribe an idealized love of self as the cure for those who suffer from mental disorders. This is understandable, since all psychologists, like all doctors and professionals, have idealized themselves and their futures in their pursuit of a graduate degree, and have been successful in the attainment of this ideal. However, this idealization of self is not an effective treatment strategy for therapants whose self-love is debilitating and who have experienced defeat and disappointment. Such therapants will usually choose, in the long run, that which they desire most, namely, the satisfaction of their concupiscible appetites or a subjective detrimental good. That is why the promotion of self-esteem and positive thinking that characterizes contemporary counseling has such dismal results. People who suffer from mental illness have seen their dreams dashed, their idealized selves and idealized futures unattainable. Those who have an idealized self-love that exceeds their natural abilities or who are prohibited by circumstances from achieving their idealized goals and requiting their idealized self-love often escape from the pain of this reality into mental disorder.

For more efficacious and enduring results, a therapant must develop a hatred of himself, that is, of his personality and the vicious aspects of his character.[6] A therapant must seek to mortify himself because he finds "himself" despicable.[7] Even in the most extreme form of the suicidal therapant, where cultivating hatred would seem contraindicated, such a therapant should learn to hate that vicious personality within him that hates his authentic self, that wishes this authentic self nonexistent. In doing so the therapant identifies with and indeed loves his authentic existent-self that is the image of God and properly expresses his hatred toward the pseudo-self that enslaves him in vice and seeks his destruction. Hatred of the pseudo-self is necessary for the therapant to begin the process of identifying with the buried imago Dei and dis-identifying with the overweening pseudo-self.

To the degree that a person undergoes this radical transformation of dying to self he will discover his true self, his *imago Dei*. He will also become open to the full range of human existence, including its gifts of joys. It is only the saints who, by the grace of God, fully enter into and transcend this realm.

Physical Mortification

Physical mortification is a volitional suffering. This process of physical mortification requires the will to break free from the emotions that dominate it

---

6 Use of the term *hate*, while uncomfortable to contemporary ears in this era of self-esteem, nonetheless has a venerable precedent in Christian asceticism that originates with Christ's own words: "[A]nyone who hates his life in this world will keep it for the eternal life" (Jn 12:25).

7 Here physical mortification, especially fasting, is most efficacious as a means of dying to one's (false) self.

and place itself under the domination of the reason. Thus physical mortification is a volitional technique. For therapants to engage in such an activity they need to possess a modicum of objectivity, an assent to reality. As such, techniques of mortification, which again require acts of volitional suffering, must often be preceded by extensive existential and cognitive techniques. Thus, physical mortification often is required before the implementation of asceticism of knowledge,[8] for a therapant is often enthralled or unduly influenced by the concupiscible appetites, the love of comfort and pleasure. In such a case, a therapant's excessive love of his own physical comfort and the obeying of his emotions must first be overcome before he can assent to and choose the highest goods.

IDP prescribes physical mortification not only as a means of gaining control over and transcending the visceral emotions of pain and pleasure, but also as a means of dying to the self-love that dominates a person with binding emotions and of facilitating the dying to self that occurs in the realm of marshaled emotions. This is because man, as an incarnate being, always has an integral connection between body and spirit. As such, the most visceral activities, such as eating, are often used to fill psychological, relational, and spiritual emptiness. At its most profound level, physical mortification facilitates the realization of one's radical contingency and vulnerability.

Physical mortification entails both the realm of practical function and the realm of essential cognition and volition. First, a therapant must recognize a higher good that is being destroyed by his following of a lower good. He must see the truth, choose it as a good, and will it, while accepting the violence subsequently done to the lower good. This strengthens his cognition (sight-of-the-truth) and his volition (striving-for-the-good). Such a task usually entails a therapant's very obvious choice to disencumber himself from the rule of an emotion and bodily sensation by placing both under the rule of reason and will.

This subordination of the emotions can be done on the level either of self-love and self-idealization or of a transcendent love that entails dying to self. As such, the Imago Dei therapist may at times seek to strengthen the will even if that means temporally utilizing a therapant's pride, self-love, and self-idealization. Thus, teaching a person to delay gratification is utilizing their self-love by having them sacrifice a lesser but more immediate

---

[8] See in chapter 8, "Striving's Mortification of the Intellect."

gratification for a greater but more remote gratification. This is a start, and in itself morally justifiable; for even in the spiritual realm it is better to obey God out of fear of damnation than to be without this fear, because this fear still recognizes the moral law and the omnipotence and justice of God.

An example of the practice of physical mortification that draws on self-love and delayed gratification would be the fasting of an overweight person. Here the higher good of health and its subsequent pleasure of feeling better can be chosen over the lower good of excessive eating with its subsequent ills. Avoiding overeating also entails reining in the emotions, since emotional succor is often the underlying good sought in this activity.

Another practice of physical mortification that draws on self-love and delayed gratification is exercise. But while there is no doubt that, for instance, a chronically depressed person would be cured if he were to engage upon a yearlong running program that culminated in his completing of a marathon, the depression itself usually prevents him from taking the first step. Many people who suffer from mental illness have concupiscible appetites so dominant and irascible appetites so weak that they do not have the fortitude to undergo habitually even a moderate regime of fasting or exercise.

Physical mortification plays an effective part at the levels of emotionality. Not only is it the remedy for those who are dominated by visceral emotions, but it is especially effective for those who are struggling to break free from binding emotions and for those who are seeking to die to idealized self-love. The effectiveness of physical mortification for those who are dominated by visceral emotions is limited by the fact that they must in some manner be coerced into its implementation, whereas those in the higher realms of emotionality can use their own volitional power to varying degrees. Physical mortification is also an effective means for achieving psychic mortification, which is the subject of the following sections.

The Silver Bullet of Psychotherapy

Contrary to what might be expected, the silver bullet of psychotherapy does not come in the form of a pill, but in the form of a virtue. The silver bullet of psychotherapy is humility. Humility is the antidote to pride; and pride is not only the primordial sin, but is also the primordial precursor of mental disorders.

Humility is a manifestation of temperance that regulates a person in his natural urge for fulfillment, superiority, preeminence, and consideration. Humility is a rational act that allows a man to form an estimation of himself according to truth.

Humility is the basis of all the virtues just as pride is the basis of all the vices. With regard to the cardinal virtues, humility is integral to prudence, for it enables one to judge himself objectively. Humility is integral to justice in expecting and rendering unto oneself, to God, and to others what is proper or due. Humility is integral to fortitude in enabling one to forgo his own subjective good for a greater good. Thus humility is a synthesizing virtue. As such, its development is of the essence of the therapeutic process.

While disorders such as narcissistic or antisocial personalities (or any of the *DSM* "Cluster B" personality disorders) are at face value the absence of humility, even personalities such as dependent, avoidant, or obsessive-compulsive (*DSM* "Cluster C" personality disorders) are, counterintuitively, caused by a lack of authentic humility. Authentic humility is not a debasement of self, but an objective appreciation of one's weaknesses and strengths. Blindness to one's strengths then is a lack of humility.

As a counterintuitive case in point, the actions of a person with a dependent personality, who may even allow others to abuse him physically, are not the actions of a humble person. Rather a dependent person that allows gratuitous abuse does so because they would rather suffer this abuse than suffer the deeper pain of rejection or abandonment. So too, the acts of someone with a dependent personality stem from being so afraid of having others dislike him that he perversely allows others to degrade him. It could be said that people with such personalities believe that everyone should like them, that they should never be disliked. It is a manifestation of a twisted pride that makes a person unable to accept the fact that he will not win the approval of all men or to understand that others do no exist for the alleviation of his insecurity.

So too, people with avoidant or schizoid personalities so fear being put down that they isolate themselves so as not to allow objective reality to intrude into their self-appraisal. They would, as it were, rather rule in the damnation of their splendid isolation, keeping intact their self-appraisal, then serve in communion with truth and accept an objective appraisal.

People with obsessive-compulsive disorders also show a lack of humility in their belief that they must have complete control, that they deserve perfection both in their world and in themselves. They cannot accept the fallen nature of the world or themselves. They cannot humbly accept the truth.

The disorder most often diagnosed and treated (usually with medication) also has its source in pride and its antidote in humility. A depressed person is not willing to accept reality and feels sorrow for himself that reality does not conform to his will. Depression is the result of reality not conforming to a person's estimation of himself or of what he deserves. If a person thinks the world owes him a living he may "just lie down and die" when he finds out it is otherwise. Of course, he may react by trying to force the world to conform to his estimation, displaying an antisocial personality. Both depression and antisocial behavior, then, have their roots in pride.

Schizophrenia, which entails chronic psychosis, is a turning away from reality. There always appears to be an event or circumstance that causes the onset of schizophrenia. Such realities are too painful for some people to accept, and thus they choose their own "reality." This psychotic "reality" always has the schizophrenic as the center of the universe, whether, for example, he suffers from a grandiose delusion such as being a god or from a paranoid delusion in which he is being followed by secret police.

The lack of humility or pride is intrinsically related to the other characteristic vices of mental illness: radical subjectivity and self-centeredness. When a person is so turned within and fixated on himself that he is able only to assent to what appeals to his own needs or that he feels the world revolves around him, he lacks an objective viewpoint. An objective viewpoint as it concerns one's person is the fruit of humility. According to St. Thomas Aquinas, "Humility in the strict sense means the awe in virtue of which man subjects himself to God" (*ST* II–II, q. 161, a. 3). This is the essential existential truth of man: his contingence, his createdness, his mortality, his nondivine status. Humility will cause a person to recognize first that he is not a god, and second that there has to be a God, a conclusion that is knowable through reason. Bringing a therapant to this dual recognition, both convincing him of its truth and persuading him of its ramifications, is a key intervention process in Imago Dei Psychotherapy.[9]

---

[9] Note that this realization of God's existence does not necessarily entail what sort of God exists (for example, the God of Judeo-Christian revelation).

Purgative Humiliation

Purgative humiliation is the result of humiliation properly embraced. Purgative humiliation produces psychic mortification; that is, psychological and spiritual mortification. This psychic mortification is the very highest form of mortification.[10] A person can become *humble* only by means of *humiliation* suffered in a purgative manner.

> Humility does not consist in a low opinion of oneself or of one's capabilities. It is not an opinion about oneself at all. As long as you are trying to think badly of yourself, you are thinking of yourself. It must not be judged on externals, in ourselves or in others. There is only one certain test of the virtue, and that is humiliation. The acceptance of humiliation alone shows the depth and reality of our humility. (Kinsella 1960, 40)

Humiliation, then, is the miraculous but fearfully painful prescription for pride and the antidote to mental illness. Humiliation is what one feels when his pride comes into contact with something that is caustic to it. Using humiliation purgatively and therapeutically dissolves pride and allows one to be open to the reality of his one infinite nothingness and God's infinite all-ness.

Bernard-Marie de Chivré, O.P. (1902–1984) wrote insightfully on the phenomenon of embracing humiliation as the essential door to wholeness and sanctity.

> It is knowing how to penetrate with holiness—gentle and at peace— into the mystery of omnipresent mediocrity, with a strength of character which does not make us flee in the weakness of a prideful solitude (taking itself for character), but on the contrary makes us dwell in the midst of mediocrity like the sun dwells in the fog: to bestow the charity of its light, and then to melt it away by the heat of its presence. It is knowing how to penetrate first of all with a mind at peace into the mystery of our own mediocrity and guilt, thinking, "Christ always passes where there are beggars." This is the strength of character which brings the Lord to

---

10 The highest form of mortification is the withdrawal of God's presence from the senses (as fully manifested in the phenomenon of the "dark night of the soul"). This spiritual mortification can be seen as the apex of humiliation, where the elect are called to completely die to self and purge themselves of all self-love that may be concomitant in their love of God.

us—the Lord loves characters which know how to persevere. Our Lord does not come to deliver us from our wretchedness, He comes to use it. (1995, choice-and-decision, 15)

Humiliation need not be curative, for it does not lead inevitably to humility. It can lead to a greater pride that is the desperate lie that masks despair. When, however, one allows the humiliation to work at dissolving his pride, he experiences purgative humiliation. How does one enter into *purgative humiliation*? And how does the Imago Dei therapist make this cure-all available to his therapant?

There are two basic types of purgative humiliation, which IDP terms *reflective humiliation* and *receptive humiliation*. The former is initiated from within, the latter imposed from without. Reflective humiliation is self-imposed; if done correctly it can be effective in reducing pride. It can also be easily misused as a means to lessen the pain of humiliation, if a person first accuses himself before another does. Receptive humiliation, on the other hand, can be endured only by a complete submission to God, for nothing of it originates with the person, who cannot even claim that he sought out the humiliation. Because of receptive humiliation's utter devastation of one's sense of self and the feeling of nothingness that it imposes upon us, it requires a turning toward God and allowance of God to love one in his utter abjectness.

The true searing fires of purgative humiliation occur only when one exercises the volitional act of accepting a humiliation that comes from without himself. If the humiliation is initiated by oneself, it does not entail a full submission to something outside of one's own powers. St. Bernard of Clairvaux (1090–1153) in his *Sermon 42 on the Canticle* describes these two types of humility:

> The one [i.e., reflective humility] has its seat in knowledge, the other in the will. If you look into yourself in the light of truth, and without dissimulation, and judge yourself unflatteringly, there is no doubt that you will be humbled, even in your own eyes; and this true knowledge of yourself will render you more vile in your own sight, although perhaps you cannot as yet endure that this be so with others. You will then be humble, but as yet only by the effect of truth, and not by the infusion of love. . . . You see then that it is not the same thing whether a man being

constrained by light and knowledge, has a low opinion of himself, and whether he is helped by the grace of charity, and willingly accepts a humble position; for the one is forced, the other voluntary. (Quoted in Kinsella 1960, 71)

In Imago Dei Psychotherapy, the psychotherapist must gently gauge the therapant's condition so as to facilitate the appropriate reflective humiliation. Oftentimes, therapants will begin therapy barely able to conjure up any elements of reflective humiliation; indeed, they are not able to identify their true faults or even, at times, any faults at all. Receptive humiliation is easily had, if not easily embraced, be it the trivial thwartings of one's will, as when one is being cut off in traffic, or devastating calamites, such as losing one's job. As a segue into receptive humiliation, the therapant reflects upon and embraces past imposed humiliation. In addition to reflective and receptive humiliation, in IDP there is also a third sort, therapeutic humiliation, which is halfway between reflective and receptive humiliation. Therapeutic humiliation is imposed from without by the psychotherapist, who takes into account the receptivity of the therapant and thus controls its content and intensity.

Before therapeutic humiliation can be imposed, the appropriate level of therapeutic rapport must be established in order for the therapant to be able to bear the pain without fearing the intent of the psychotherapist; that is, knowing that the humiliation is imposed with only the good of the therapants in mind with no vicious intent. If therapeutic humiliation is imposed too soon or to too great a degree, a therapant develops animosity toward the psychotherapist or terminates therapy completely. Yet therapeutic humiliation is of the essence of IDP psychotherapy, for here the therapant encounters the existential truth that shatters personality defenses and creates a waxing openness-to-reality. So too in therapeutic humiliation the supernatural realm that St. Bernard alludes to in the above quotation begins to be touched upon, if merely to salve the emptiness that is the result of the psychotherapeutic intervention. In therapeutic humiliation psychotherapy begins to enter into the twilight between body and soul. Here the psychotherapist is the precursor to the spiritual director.

As with humiliation in general, there are three possible responses to this therapeutic humiliation. The first is for the therapant to open himself up to the fullness of reality. Here he is open to all reality, physical and spiritual, and is positioned to take a leap of faith into the all-loving embrace of God.

Or he may not have the courage to leap into the Infinite, but instead, left with the half-truth of his own nothingness, stands paralyzed in fixation on the black void of his own existence. In this latter case a spiritual pride can be resurrected that proclaims, "If I am nothing, then all is nothing," and thus a person bitterly and grudgingly refuses to worship or even acknowledge the Supreme Being. Or, and this seems to be the most prevalent propensity, a person impelled by self-love scampers back from the precipice of existence and returns to his distractions, defenses, and analgesics.

These three responses, respectively, are the hot, the cold, and the lukewarm of which Christ speaks. It is well then, if a therapist can facilitate a change in a therapant's temperature from lukewarm to cold, for at least then that therapant is so positioned as to take an authentic leap of faith. The despair and bitterness that is entailed in the cold therapant's half-truth of nothingness is grist for the therapeutic mill, and with but a final milling of humiliation, the addition of the leaven of faith, and the application of the heat of charity, a therapant will have his hunger filled with the hope that is found in the fullness of reality.

Humiliation then is requisite for humility, and humility, as both the precursor to and the result of openness-to-reality, enables a person to accept the full spectrum of human existence, both the sorrows and the joys. When, in addition, a person accepts the truth of divine revelation, he also gains the courage to embrace wholly these sorrows and joys. He can then bear the full yoke of human existence, which is the key to the peace of soul that best assures mental health:

> Take up my yoke upon you, and learn of me, because I am meek and humble of heart; and you shall find rest to your souls. (Mt 11:29)

Suffering-Well

Suffering—physically, psychologically, and spiritually—is the sine qua non of human existence. The promise of Imago Dei Psychotherapy is not to alleviate this suffering, but rather to allow a therapant to suffer-well and gain peace of mind and soul. As mentioned before, the psychological term "angst" (existential anxiety) may find its ultimate origin in the Latin *angustiae*, which means "narrowing or straits." Angst may also facilitate a widening and opening. The German use of the term angst appears to have etymological connotations of childbirth. The pain of childbirth is often reacted to as a purely negative phenomenon, as a painful constricting that is to be fought or anesthetized. However, in reality the pain is a positive manifestation of the birthing process.

A proven psychological technique for lessening the pangs of childbirth is to visualize the uterus as the hollow cylindrical muscle that it is, and thus functioning according to design when it contracts and opens up. When this is done, a woman can accept and relax with the uterine contractions because she understands that the pain is a good and healthy pain and not to be feared and fought. By her accepting and "going with" the contractions as opposed to fearing and fighting them, the pain is lessened and the uterine contractions of the birthing process are facilitated.

As in childbirth, where the uterine muscle constricts painfully so that the cervix effaces or opens up to allow birth, so too pain accompanies a person's progressing through the three levels of emotionality, the three zones of mental health, and a greater openness-to-reality. This pain is to be embraced as the essential accompaniment of human growth. The pain and the suffering, then, inherent in human existence are not to be avoided or fought, but rather to be accepted and used as a catalyst for growth.

CHAPTER **10**

● ● ●

IDP's Spiritual Elements

T HE EXPLORATION of existential concerns necessarily involves the exploration of religious belief. Thus, religious exploration is part and parcel of Imago Dei Psychotherapy's existential technique, where the therapant is brought for the first time or once again to the existential chasm of choice. The choice demanded by this gaze upon the void is either to face a soul-searing encounter with existence or to scamper back from reality. In the process, it is not doubt that is facilitated but rather an honest reevaluation of what one actually believes. This involves the drawing out of belief, where inconsistencies or logical disconnects between asserted belief and practiced belief (in both morals and coping), between a therapant's formal and ideal worldview and his core or functional belief, are made manifest. By facilitating a brutally honest appraisal of his faith, a therapant is helped to know exactly where he is in his faith and thus gain integrity of faith.

The Existence of God

An essential principle of IDP is that the existence of God can be known through the use of reason alone. The Church teaches *de fide*, "If anyone shall say that the One true God, our Creator and Lord, cannot be certainly known by the natural light of human reason through created things, let him be anathema."[1] One might argue that a position of atheism is a manifestation of a disordered cognitive or mental state; that is, it is unreasonable to conclude there is no God, for it is nothing less than a probabilistic

---

[1] *Dei Filius,* First Vatican Council, Session 3, Can. 1.

absurdity to believe that there is no intelligent design behind the universe. At the same time, it is important to realize that because of the privileged position of the psychotherapist and the power differential between him and the therapant, there is a chance of coercion and the danger of the therapist supplanting by the force of persuasion what is to be a free act of faith on part of the therapant (see "The Pietistic Persona" below).

This natural knowledge of God is not an innate knowledge, but one that needs proof.[2] Thus, it is part of a Catholic psychotherapy to facilitate a therapant's knowledge of God's existence through the use of reason. Indeed, this process may be considered a hallmark of IDP technique. In practice this knowledge may at times result only in a therapant's knowing that there must be an "eternal principle" (a principle that he and all men intrinsically seek) and that this "eternal principle" does not consist of himself or the created universe.

At best, even when a man knows with unaided reason that God exists in all His perfection, this nonetheless does not tell him who that God is and, most relevantly, whether that God cares for him. So while reason suffices to tell us that God is, faith tells us *who* God is; beyond the mere *reasonable conclusion* that there is a God, there is the *faith belief* in the Triune God of Revelation, which is a gift. The same council that declared the existence of God knowable through unaided reason likewise declared: "If anyone shall say that in divine revelation there are no mysteries, truly and properly so called, but that all the doctrines of faith can be understood and demonstrated from natural principles, by properly cultivated reason, let him be anathema." The competency and concern of the IDP psychotherapist would be to lead the therapant up to the point of mystery and faith. Again, this does not mean that God is not to be spoken of, but quite the contrary, that He is to be discussed so that the therapant assents via reason to His existence and evident qualities.

Faith is not a faulty faculty of man, or one that is inferior to reason, but rather man's highest faculty. Man was meant to believe, for it is by faith that he comes to view the infinity of truth that his limited intellect by reason alone is unable to grasp. It is by way of faith that he becomes divinized.[3]

---

[2] Tanquerey 1959, 251.

[3] Man can either humbly and rightly seek to know God or pridefully seek to know what God knows; the former entails sanctification or divinization where the latter entails damnation.

There are two aspects of true faith: God's proffering of it and man's acceptance of it. Whereas the explication of the former is the competency of sacred theology, the explication of the latter is the competency of both sacred theology and psychology. For having faith, receiving the gift, is not a one-time event, as most non-Catholic Christians would assert, but an ongoing volitional choice to accept the gift. The process of being reborn is not a singular isolated event in time, but rather a process that is meant to last a lifetime. As J. R. R. Tolkien once said, faith is "a permanent and indefinitely repeated act rather than a momentous, final decision." God knocks, and He may even open the door and hand man the gift of faith; however, man must acquiesce to this opening and this gift, and the act of acquiescing ends only with death. This acquiescing is a response to God's promptings that is not passive but volitionally receptive.

Some Protestants see man's free will, in effect, as being taken away or mitigated once he accepts Christ (once one is "saved" he cannot reject Christ), and thus the "born-again" becomes spiritually staid or set. Catholicism, on the other hand, sees man's free will coming more and more into play, becoming stronger and stronger, as he engages in the continual process of being born, as he grows in faith. This leads, not to a spiritual staidness, a point of equilibrium, but to an ever-increasing spiritual drama, which in the saints is often characterized by the tragic dark night of the soul. It is when faith believes beyond hope, in this very dark night of the soul, that free will reaches its heights and a person loves God in the purest manner.

It is thus within the competency of a Catholic psychology to help a therapant give his "yes" to God; to what that "yes" is an answer to is more in the realm of spiritual direction than of psychology. IDP's existential job, then, is to prepare the therapant for and lead him to the chasm of faith. Although it is a twilight transition, it is at this chasm that Catholic psychology and philosophy (representing the two facets of reason) fall away, giving way to spirituality, grace, and mysticism.

A Reasonable Faith

Although faith transcends reason, it should not be unreasonable. As such, faith beliefs can be challenged therapeutically. Such a challenge, when done appropriately, gently facilitates the therapant's examination of his own beliefs.

The tenets of faith can be examined directly by a psychotherapist, but great care must be taken to avoid any conveyance of his own beliefs. More appropriately and importantly, the logical consistency of a therapant's beliefs can be examined. For example, a suicidal therapant may say that his death will end all his suffering, but when queried may express belief in God and in the consequences of eternal punishment. In such a case, his religious belief has not permeated his thinking or actions even when it is a moral question of life and death.

Strengthening the rationality and logical consistency of a therapant's faith only increases the quality of that faith. Just as grace builds upon nature, faith builds upon reason and results in wisdom. "Fear of the Lord [the horizon, the context of faith] is the beginning of wisdom" (Prov 111:10). It can also be said to be the beginning of sanity. Fear of the Lord has its foundations in natural reason and is the realization of God's Almightiness and His complete Otherness, and of one's creaturehood and complete contingency. This realization, this fear, is the result of humility; and the humble realization of limitations ("in weakness I am strong") and the honest assessment of potential is the key to mental health.

An act of faith is a reasonable act,[4] an intellectual assent to the truth, that transcends reason by going through it as a means. Reason is what separates faith from wishful thinking and fantasy. Reason is what validates true religious belief, the paradigm of which is found in Catholic belief, and exposes superstition and false religion. Reason helps convey revelation via speculative philosophy. Reason, in the form of proper metaphysical constructs, orients the mind toward the transcendent. Deprived of reason, faith stresses feeling and experience, and so runs the risk of becoming purely subjective and losing its quality as a universal proposition.

God can also be known through His creation through unaided reason. Knowing God, specifically that He exists, through empirical observation is a completely natural phenomenon, although it should lead to seeking the God of Revelation. The natural knowing of God redounds back upon reason and enhances it by placing all other knowledge in its proper context and synthesizing it in accord with the integral divine design.

---

[4] Though an *act of faith* utilizes reason, it is dependent upon *infused faith*, which is a gift of God and which can exist without the use of reason. For instance, a person possessed of infused faith without the use of reason is the case of a baptized infant.

The sundering of *faith from reason* results in either a radical rationalism that leads to skepticism because reason is insufficient in itself or to an idealism where reason overrides faith.[5] The sundering of *reason from faith* leads either to agnosticism as a reaction to the production of irrational or absurd beliefs or to fideism, where faith overrides or dismisses reason. Faith and reason have a circular relationship, each nourishing and being nourished by the other. There cannot be authentic faith without reason or right reason without faith.

The Pietistic Persona

The Imago Dei integration of scientific technique into the Catholic worldview clearly defines the specific competencies of psychotherapy and spiritual direction. Unlike efforts at non-Catholic integration, the Church has as the essence of its spiritual life the sacramental system which is intrinsically tied to the office of the priesthood. As such, spiritual direction/ministry in its fullness is a competency of the priesthood.

This demarcation helps avoid one of the major pitfalls inherent in "Christian psychotherapy," that of the *pietistic persona*. Such a persona is a pious mask that is presented to the outside world and to the community of believers and is to some degree inauthentic or in excess of the depths of a person's faith. It is especially prevalent in those denominations that consider a person either "saved" or "predestined," which is authenticated by how they act and/or how prosperous they are. When a therapant hides behind such a persona, it impedes or prevents therapeutic progress. When a therapist himself displays overt signs of piety—for example, by prayer (especially nonformulaic prayer) before or during a session, by Bible readings, or by sermonettes—a therapant may react by meeting the expectations of the therapist or mirroring the therapist's piety by himself adopting in the therapeutic relation a pietistic persona. Of course, a therapant may have such a persona outside of the clinic as well, but that should be made manifest with no promptings from the therapist. If the majority of psychological disorders have their roots in existential concerns, then the therapant must be willing to bare such concerns even though they appear incongruous with his overt religious belief or demonstration.

---

[5] Idealism is inclusive of many "isms," such as scientism. See in chapter 4, "Epistemological Distortions."

Peace of Soul

Civilization and technology help alleviate the brutalizing impact of physical existence. Warmth, food, and leisure allow man to look beyond the struggle for existence to the meaning of existence. As such, as the physical ills of man are decreased, his psychic ills are increased. As man's physical existence becomes more secure, his existential angst becomes more severe.

So too, the further a society distances itself from the immediate demands of nature the greater its population's chance of losing an innate sense of natural law. The hunter-gatherer or the agricultural cultures are intimately tied to nature and its exigencies and thus to reality. The more a culture becomes immune from the exigencies of nature the fewer "reality checks" it has. Even in the middle ages, St. Thomas Aquinas was lamenting the loss of a sense of the natural law among the populace who had begun to live in villages.

Man is not going against the punitive consequences imposed by God in Genesis or against the command of Christ to take up the cross when he seeks to lessen the physical burdens and ills of life. He is *elevating this burden to a psychic level, to a more and more human level.* Man is a rational being, and ills of the mind/soul are ills most human. Because of man's inherently deficient and limited nature as a creature and corporal being and because of the effects of original sin he will always experience physical and psychic suffering. This is why a Catholic psychology such as Imago Dei Psychotherapy finds its final goal not in escaping psychic suffering, for to do so would be an escape from reality, but in embracing this suffering in a growth-producing way.

Even if a person is not imminently threatened with or actually in pain, the world is filled with suffering, and death stalks all men. Not to be cognizant of and open to such suffering through empathy and foresightedness is to be closed-off to one's fellow men and to one's own nature as a being who is inherently contingent and fragile. IDP's final end, then, is to allow a therapant to accept and respond to reality; to bear the burdens, sorrows, anxieties, and sufferings of this life with peace; and to find a creative catalyst in that suffering.

To the extent that a person is open to and embraces the sorrows of human existence, so too is he open to and embraces the joys of human existence. Man fears to live fully, for he fears the intensity of the sorrow and hence may forfeit the intensity of the joy. When a person succumbs to this fear he seeks a lukewarm existence. Such cowardice, such a failure to live fully, is a common neurosis that is endemic in the modern West's ethos of materialism and moderate hedonism, of room temperature comfort and compromise.

Dasein-in-Christ

The Imago Dei's psychotherapeutic process is painful, for it entails bringing the therapant to accept the pain of his existence. So too, IDP requires therapeutic challenging as part of convincing a therapant of the objective truth, the falsity of his subjective thinking, and persuading him to strive for that truth and reject that falsity. However, both the acceptance of the pain and therapeutic challenging first requires that therapeutic rapport be firmly established. In Imago Dei Psychotherapy, such a rapport is called Dasein-in-Christ.[6]

As mentioned throughout this treatise, it is a lack of openness to truth that is the hallmark of both mental illness and sin. As such, a therapant is usually both hypersensitive to pain and criticism and unmoved by them due to built-up defenses. It is crucial then that the Imago Dei psychotherapist must build a deep rapport by encountering the therapant Dasein-in-Christ. This rapport takes place in the Realm of the Preconscious (see chapter 8), as such it is an openness-to-reality that encounters the therapant's as being-as-such, in the image of God, and as a saint in potentia. So while therapeutic intervention may be arduously taking place in the Realms of Cognition and Volition, the Preconscious encounter Dasein-in-Christ remains; indeed, it is the motivation and relational dynamics behind all therapeutic intervention. Thus the Imago Dei therapist values in each therapant an intrinsic worth that transcends the therapant's particular woundedness or even viciousness, knowing that whatsoever he does to the least of his brothers he does unto Christ.

Imago Dei's Dasein-in-Christ therapeutic relationship does not merely value the therapant "as is," but rather views him as Christ does: as a saint in potentia. Man, made in the image of God, exists to know, love, and serve Him in this world and behold the beatific vision in eternity. Through the efficacy of Christ's sacrifice and the administration of the

---

[6] See also in chapter 5, "Therapeutic Relationship Factors."

sacrament of baptism, man is made capable of sanctification. Although an Imago Dei therapist would not implement faith content into sessions with a nonbeliever, he nonetheless prepares the way for faith and subsequent sanctification by his rectification of the natural man in accord with the anthropology of the Church. Although an Imago Dei therapist must be prudent in preaching the Gospel to his therapants due to the intrinsic danger of coercive and thus inauthentic conversion, he nonetheless knows that God desires an authentic conversion of all men.

Dasein-in-Christ also sees the therapant as a unique unrepeatable person, who is ultimately nondissectible and nonquantifiable. In recognizing that every person is created in God's image, the Imago Dei therapist sees each person as sharing in God's infinite unfathomability and mystery. Imago Dei psychotherapy seeks to preserve the dignity, modesty, and mystery of the person. Intrinsic to this preservation is the holding that there is a type of shame that is both healthy and therapeutic. Because of man's existential contingency, he experiences an intrinsic inadequacy. Because of original and actual sin, which causes man to be intrinsically disordered, he experiences perversity in his nature. Shame is the recognition of the inadequacy inherent in human contingency and is not only a safeguard against the expansion of the disorder of sin, but an antidote as well.

Imago Dei's therapeutic preservation and facilitation of healthy shame is quite contrary to the practices of professional psychology, which holds that unbridled self-disclosure is the key to therapeutic success. From the classic psychoanalytic goal of uncovering all of an analysand's deepest and most perverse desires, to the encounter group's expectation and pressure on members to fully disclose the most personal of matters to erstwhile strangers, to the desensitization techniques of sex education programs—the mechanism is the same: the destruction of the sense of shame. It is not surprising then, and is a backhanded compliment, that according to Freudian clinical folklore, Catholics (at least those of a bygone era) are the ethnic group most resistant to psychoanalysis due to their strong super-ego.[7]

A *Dasein*-in-Christ relationship is not one way. The psychotherapist not only must encounter the therapant authentically but must present himself to the therapant authentically. This does not mean he must disclose per-

---

[7] Freud viewed the super-ego as the locus of religious belief and viewed religion itself as a "universal neurosis."

sonally. On the contrary, it is advisable that the IDP therapist always maintain a bearing that is conducive to his office as a doctor of psychology or, if not a doctor, as a psychotherapist who is commissioned to carry out the work of the profession of psychology.[8] This provides appropriate boundaries. It also produces an efficacious tension that allows the therapist to give his heart to a therapant while at the same time maintaining a professional relationship that seeks no emotional recompense. This professional office, as an office, although of the essence of the therapeutic relationship, is not of the essence of the psychotherapist's person. What then does it mean for a psychotherapist to be authentically present to a therapant in the *Dasein*-in-Christ relationship? It means the psychotherapist recognizing this difference of office and person, while at the same time recognizing the wretchedness of himself. St. Thérèse of Lisieux said this about a person's relationship with Christ: *"If you are willing to bear serenely the trial of being displeasing to yourself, then you will be for Jesus a pleasant place of shelter."* This applies as well to a person's relationship with others, and to a psychotherapist's relationship with his therapants. If a therapist is humble in his person, in touch with his wretchedness, and professional in his commissioning as a healer of souls, then he will indeed be a pleasant place of shelter for his therapants because Christ will abide with him.

The Communal Nature of Man

The pivotal dogmas of original sin and the Redemption are based on this communal reality: "[A]s truly as men would not be born unjust, if they were not born through propagation of the seed of Adam . . . , so if they were not born again in Christ, they would never be justified" (*Decrees of the Council of Trent*, Session VI). The radical communality of these doctrines is further reflected in the Church's teachings on the mystical body of Christ and on the communion of saints, and in her holding that infants can be

---

[8] A simple way to do this is to use the title "Doctor," or, in the case of the nondoctoral therapist, to be called by Mister, Miss, or Mrs. So too, professional dress is important. What G. K. Chesterton said about Thomas Beckett *[sic]* applies to the role of the psychologist: "He wore a hair shirt under his gold and crimson, and there is much to be said of the combination; for Beckett *[sic]* got the benefit of the hair shirt while the people on the street got the benefit of the crimson and gold."

validly baptized by the consent of others. The mystery of the Trinity reveals God Himself to be absolutely communal: three distinct Persons in one God.

So too, the field of psychology acknowledges the communal nature of man and the social etiology of much of mental illness. In particular, it acknowledges the elementary social unit of the family as that which is the most essential factor in mental health. It is in the family that the child experiences his psychic birth, internalizes values, and undergoes his crucial development. It is in the family that the child is meant to experience his closest of relationships, the irreplaceable love of his parents toward him. Many theories of psychotherapy hold that psychotherapy is but an attempt to re-parent, or to undo and repair that which occurred in a therapant's family of origin.

Imago Dei Psychotherapy also holds that there is a familial etiology to most psychopathology. The premium that both clinical psychology (especially, and almost across the board, personality theories) and Catholicism place on the family makes it the crucial milieu and locus of etiology for mental, moral, and societal ills. A Catholic clinical psychology should go beyond the mere recognition of the family etiology of much mental illness and prescribe the norms and dynamics of a healthy, holy family.

It is in the family that a person is or should be allowed to be his authentic, spontaneous self; where he can love, laugh, mourn, and dream without fear that his unguarded and vulnerable heart will be trampled upon. It is in the family that a person should be able to drop all pretense and engage in authentic relationships. It is in the family that life should be most fully lived in all its joys and sorrows. It is the familial setting that is the "real world." So too, it is in the family that a child receives that unconditional yet demanding love that imbues him with a transcendent sense of worth and dignity that finds its locus not in self but in God. It is in the family that a child is loved not for what he does but for who he is. This sense that one's being has intrinsic worth is not to be confused with a prideful self-esteem, for it allows one to evaluate oneself critically while still maintaining a sense of worth that transcends and, instead of glossing over, accentuates one's faults.

As un-politically correct as the past emphasis of predominate personality theories on the "bad mother" as the source of psychic maladjustment was, it is nonetheless the mother who is most crucial for imbuing the child with the unconditional love that is crucial for his transcendent sense of worth. The mother, then, can be said to have the crucial developmental impact, for good or ill, on the psychological development of the child. So too, the legendary effects of the "fatherless home" witness to the need for a strong father to complete the wholesome development of the child, especially in the realm of socialization.

Although outside the scope of this treatise, the place of marital/family therapy in the Imago Dei armamentarium is of utmost importance. Subsidiarity, the locating of responsibility and intervention at the most elementary unit, is an honored principle of the Catholic Church. As such, what can be rectified at the family level should be. Marital/family therapy is also the one area that deals directly with a religious entity; in the case of Catholicism, it deals with nothing less than a sacrament.

However, because most therapants come to clinic after childhood, family therapy is often not possible. As such, therapy often entails a certain reparenting that attempts to rectify that which has its etiology in the family of origin. Such a rectification, however, does not allow a therapant to wallow in the past, but is aimed at breaking free from it by facilitating the realization that the therapant need not be a victim of his past, but rather can be the author of his future.

Faith, Reason, and Existentialism

Faith is that which allows man to transcend the limits of his intellect. Without faith man is trapped in the dungeon of his own reasoning ability, which cannot fathom existence, but rather redounds upon itself in confusion and results in absurdity. For man in his self-reflection finds that he by himself has no principle of existence, of self-creation. In order to break out of this prison of self-ratification, man must look beyond himself for the reason of existence. It is only by faith that he can look beyond himself. The essential existential dilemma of man ethologically comprises him as a creature of faith.

The existential question, then, is a religious question. Man either abandons his prideful self-reliance on his intellectual capacities and opens himself up to the vistas of faith or he wallows in the dungeon of his darkened intellect. The faith-filled man uses all his faculties and is truly free when he becomes actualized in the infinity of God. The faithless man is trapped, and at best can only substitute for faith "engagements" that are the counterfeit and self-deceptive distractions created by the mind for temporal respite from the crushing absurdity of existence. The existential question is the essential question; indeed, it is the human question. *It is the capacity for faith.* Without it one cannot have true faith.

Man has only two options: to be either a nihilist or a theist. Those who do not entertain the existential question are the lukewarm, who not only distract themselves with mundane engagements, but make faith itself a mundane engagement, something that is a comfort and distraction from the existential dilemma. Of course, even the confirmed nihilist admits of engaging in distraction; otherwise he would have implemented his final and only choice not to exist, even if this is but the suicidal distraction of "burning the candle at both ends." The theist himself often uses his faith or a rendition of it for mundane distraction instead of being challenged by it. Faith is not primarily for comfort but rather for growth, which entails pain and uneasiness. The fact that faith allows one to enter fully into the mystery of existence, to plummet with life's sorrows and soar with its joys, is more aptly described as courageous rather than comfortable.

So far from authentic faith being "an opiate," it acts to sensitize a person to and to actualize his capacity for the fullness of life. Faith allows a person to embrace, or enter deeply into, the pain and suffering of existence. Faith allows a person to realize fully and accept even death and one's radical contingence and thus also allows one to embrace fully the joys of life. Faith gives a person the courage and capacity to give and accept love fully: the love for others, the love of others, and most of all the love for and of God, a love that literally keeps man in existence.

False Faith

When one reduces the faith to a fideism, a faith without reason, one does not take the intellect seriously enough, does not embrace the existential question and the looming absurdity of a life without faith. Contrary to fideism's Latin etymon *fide* (faith), fideism does not call for true faith at all. True faith reaches out from man's intellect, as limited as that intellect may be. To the extent that one embraces the existential experience, which is an experience of questioning, one acquires the capacity for and is deposed toward faith.

While theism, or belief in a Supreme Being, is the only non-nihilistic answer to the existential question, Christ is the only fully adequate and therefore fully liberating answer. It is in embracing Christ crucified that the existential question is fully embraced. To *embrace* something is to experience it fully but not necessarily to understand it fully. One can never fully understand the infinite and unfathomable God, although the beatific vision is the ever-waxing eternal process of understanding and loving God. Much less can one understand God's becoming man and His immolation. But one can experience God in Christ crucified by embracing Him through one's own sufferings. In this manner man is able to be on the most intimate terms with God: the most intimate terms of suffering and dying. Indeed, the most dramatic day of a person's life is the day of his death. Physiologically one goes through the most strenuous of all activities. Emotionally one plumbs his heart. Spiritually one is acutely aware of his own contingency as he is about to face the Noncontingent.

The true theist is not one who is immune to existential anguish or who is not engulfed in the seeming absurdity of life. He is not one who can look upon the face of death and not have his mind thrown into confusion and his heart pierced with debilitating anguish. The true theist lives with this apparent absurdity but does not measure existence by it. The absurdity is but a manifestation of man's createdness, of his limitedness, of his non-self-sufficiency. Without apparent absurdity as a product of a limited intellect man would not need faith, and without faith man must be trapped in absurdity.

The true theist realizes his nothingness and contingency and therefore appreciates God's "allness" and necessity. This is the human tension, where every fiber of man's being is taut and thus resounds with the music of existence as man experiences it. The nihilist strives to snap these fibers, although he can never do so completely, and even the death he believes to be an annihilation will fail to do so. The lukewarm theist loosens these fibers so that not a sound resounds. Yes, rather "one hot or cold, than lukewarm," for even the fraying and breaking fibers of the nihilist, though greatly reduced in range of scale, are able to resound with the sound of existence, even if this sound is but the twang of snapping strings. God can turn a discord into the first note of a new symphony. Not so with the lukewarm, who refuses to feel the tension of his existence but would rather live a life without music so long as it is without tensions.

Man is meant for faith. It is that which allows him to be divinized. Man can either humbly seek to know God or pridefully covet to know what God knows; the former entails sanctification or divinization, where the latter entails damnation.

Sin, Evil, and the Demonic

The Imago Dei clinician has a vested interest in the spiritual status of his therapant because that status impacts directly on the therapant's psychological status. Sin, both original and actual, causes psychological (and physical) impairment. The Imago Dei clinician also recognizes that psychological health impacts a therapant's spiritual status, providing the cultivated ground necessary for the fruitful reception of the seed of faith and its subsequent growth.

Clinical psychology often deals with the effects of sin, be that sin original or actual. These effects, impairment of the intellect and will, not only flow from sin, but can facilitate sin. Sin is spiritual ill. In that the remittance of original sin via baptism does not remove the effects of original sin, and repentance/absolution does not automatically remove the habits of or affection for sin, clinical psychology deals with these effects. Indeed, the remedying of the effects is gravely important, for these effects can lead once again to sin. The effects of sin are recorded in the character and must be erased or rewritten, the doing of which delineates respectively the competency of the spiritual director/confessor and the Imago Dei clinician.

Finally, it must be noted again that though sinfulness impacts sanity, sanity does not equal sanctity. Vladimir Soloviev (1853–1900) writes of the coming Antichrist as one who will be "a man of irreproachable morals and exceptional genius" (1915), but whose self-love and pride is immeasurable. The truly evil man or evil genius is quite sane functionally, and perpetrates his schemes quite rationally. He is well able to delay gratification, choose higher goods over lower, but always in service of himself. When confronted with the choice of serving God he fails, even if it is only after death when in a fit of rage and pride he rejects God Almighty in favor of the torturous isolation of hell, where he can be his own eternally damned god.

Imago Dei

The Blessed Virgin Mary completely lived her human existence in all its sorrow, joy, and peace. She always responded "yes" to God, whether it was to the incomparable joy of His incarnation in her womb, or to the consummate sorrow of His sacrifice on the Cross, or to the supreme glory of His resurrection. It was Mary alone who shared most intimately in the Passion of Good Friday; hence it was Mary alone who rejoiced most fully in the triumph of Easter Sunday.[9]

As God's Immaculate Mother, Mary lived a life most deeply, truly, and fully human. What unimaginable joys she experienced holding and suckling her God and Savior! With what infinite and ever-expanding joy she was filled when her divine baby gazed into her eyes and smiled and cooed with all the love of He who is love! And what unfathomable, glorious joy was hers at the first moments[10] of His Resurrection.

Nor was there ever one who partook in Christ's suffering as she did. It was she whom Our Lord asked in response to her request for wine at the Wedding of Cana, "What is it to thee and to me?" that is, "What is it to us?" thus showing the intimate bond of His suffering and hers. Then, in honor of her motherhood and in consideration of the passion she would suffer with Him, He graciously submitted to her intercession that hastened His and her journey to Golgotha though His hour had "not yet come." As mother and son, creature and Creator, silently gazed into each other's eyes and the depth of the coming passion was made known, she once again gave her "yes" to God's will, though it pierced her very heart: "Whatsoever he shall say to you, do ye" (Jn 2:5). And so it came to pass that just as it was Our Lady's privilege to share in Our Lord's first steps toward His sacrificial death on the Cross, it was her privilege to receive Him into her maternal arms after all had been accomplished.

It is the Blessed Virgin Mary, full of peace and grace, who is united with God the Father as obedient daughter, with God the Holy Spirit as devoted spouse, and with God the Son as loving mother. By following holy Mary's example and availing oneself of her maternal embrace, one is able to say

[9] The Blessed Virgin Mary's union with her Son and Lord Jesus Christ in His passion was so complete that many theologians and popes have given her the title of "Co-Redemptrix." Not only did her *compassion* make her one with the passion of Christ crucified, but it was she who gave Him the enfleshment necessary for that sacrifice.

[10] It is the constant tradition of the Church that the Risen Savior first appeared to His Mother Mary on Easter Sunday. And what else explains His scripturally unaccounted for initial absence that first Easter morning? Surely, the event was meant to remain a mystery because it is too glorious for mortal men to comprehend; indeed, if this author may so surmise, Our Lady beheld the beatific vision on earth!

"yes" to the vicissitudes of existence and thus die to the self-love and pride that disfigures the image of God that is one's authentic self. In and through her Son, the Blessed Virgin Mary models for us the human image of God: for from her His humanity is singularly taken, and in her His divinity is pristinely partaken.

● ● ●

Seven Principles of Imago Dei Psychotherapy

THE FOLLOWING seven general theoretical principles are deemed essential to Imago Dei Psychotherapy. Following each principle is a brief explanation and the location of its detailed account.

1. *IDP is Thomistic, existential, and psychodynamic.*
   Thomism provides the anthropology of IDP, its teleology, its episte-mology, and its understanding of the moral act (chapters 2, 3, 4, 8). Thomism, as a philosophy of being or existence, also provides the existential basis of IDP. The existential orientation of IDP recognizes that man is a "seeker of truth," and the ultimate questions of life, death, love, and meaning underlie anxiety (chapter 5). Because IDP utilizes a definitive anthropology, it is psychodynamic; that is, it claims to know the underlying dynamics of human action. IDP's psy-chodynamics is further explicated in its theory of personality, where personality is the defensive secretion of self-love and pride against the pain of reality (chapters 7–9).

2. *IDP defines mental health as the ability to perceive, receive, reflect upon, and act upon the real. Man can be essentially defined as a seeker of truth.* Man's specific difference is his reason, and his reason is made to assent to truth (capax verum) (chapter 4). When the rational image of the mind (that which is in God's image) is restored, it is capable of achieving its end, which is truth. In that all created reality, all truth, leads man to the knowledge of God, who is the final end of man, full mental health entails the natural assent of reason to the existence of God (chapter 10).

3. *IDP espouses an epistemology of realism and implements a clinical eval-uation that is both inductive and deductive.*

   Epistemology is of utmost importance to IDP because IDP defines mental health as the ability to perceive, receive, reflect upon, and act upon the real. Truth is the real in cognitive terms. Some of the key holdings of Thomistic conceptual realism fulfill the need for an episte-mology of realism: that man's faculties are purposeful and therefore made to perceive and reflect upon the world accurately; that truth is arrived at both empirically and philosophically; that there must be cer-titude in the cognitive connection between empirical experience and revealed truth (chapter 4). Thomistic epistemology also allows for both deductive and inductive arrival at knowledge. Clinical induction begins with particular symptomology and ends with general diagnostic catego-rization, while clinical deduction begins with general anthropological principles and ends with particular etiological conclusions (chapter 4).

4. *IDP personality theory identifies vices and virtues to be, respectively, the catalysts and remedies of characterological and mental disorder.*

   Because of the Church's divine insight into human nature, her moral-ity and anthropology are normative for all men. The science of psy-chology's realm of competency is limited to the natural realm, and moral living and adherence to natural law is an essential component of any therapy. Although grace builds upon nature, nature does not encompass the supernatural realm. Clinical psychology properly deals only with the characterological residue of sin. Spiritual intervention is an ecclesiological competency, but various effects of both original and actual sin remain after sacramental remittance. These effects of sin disorder the will and darken the intellect (chapters 3, 4, 10).

5. *IDP's theory of psychotherapy utilizes the Thomistic conceptualization of the person as a moral agent as outlined in the Moral Agency Schema.*

   The Moral Agency Schema demarcates reason and free will to be of the essence of the person and, as such, necessary for an authentically human/moral act. As a result, IDP psychotherapeutic intervention impacts rationality and volition, and is essentially aimed at strength-ening and ordering the will, the intellect's ability to assent to truth, and facilitating a greater existential openness-to-reality (chapter 8).

6. *IDP conceptualizes psychological diagnostics and the degree of mental health as integrally related to the corresponding continuums of the tripartite faculties of the soul.*

Man is an integral being whose mental health, moral agency, reason, and volition are all integrally united, determined, and governed by his soul (chapter 6).

7. *IDP is ordered toward restoring the image of God in the therapant.*

Man is created in imago Dei, and as such is a moral agent whose specific difference is his rational ability to assent to truth and his volitional ability to love and attain that truth as a good. Each person is recognized as unique and remains in essence an unfathomable mystery, for man, being created in God's image, shares in His infinite unfathomability (chapters 1–10).

APPENDIX B

● ● ●

The Psychovitiation
of Catholicism

THE DANGER of a psychology severed from the sure guidance of Catholic philosophy and theology resides not only in the delicate quasi-spiritual nature of its subject matter (the mind) and in the hubris that is scientism, but with psychology's tendency, because of this subject matter, to supplant religion and spirituality. Indeed, as many critics of modern psychology have noted, it has often become its own religion. When the spirit of Catholicism is removed from the equation, other spirits move in. In a highly secularized culture, and an even more secularized profession, these spirits are usually hostile toward the erstwhile Catholic ones. It is largely by means of an insinuating secular psychology that Catholics have been secularized.

The unprecedented devastation of Catholic religious orders, of priestly vocations, of traditional parish life, one can even argue the great secular apostasy of the twentieth century itself, was spearheaded by a *psychovitiation* that gradually usurped traditional Catholic spirituality. It is psychology's ability to ape authentic spirituality that allows it to insinuate slyly itself into religious life. Humanistic psychology, most especially group therapy and sensitization training, was the Trojan horse that would gain access to the inner sanctums of the Faith in order to spew forth its diabolical poison. A case in point is William Coulson's (1994) repentant tale of the Rogerian destruction of one vibrant teaching order of nuns through group therapy.

In fact, the case of the Immaculate Heart of Mary nuns is so tragically emblematic of the negative influence of psychology upon the Church that a brief account is in order. William Coulson, who was Carl Rogers's right-hand man in his insidious mission to the IHM nuns of Los Angeles, has repentantly described the damage. What follows is an abbreviated account:

> I met with the whole community, some 600 nuns gathered in the Immaculate Heart High School gymnasium, in Hollywood, on an April day in 1967. We've already done the pilot study, we told them. Now we want to get everybody in the system involved in nondirective self-exploration. We call it encounter groups, but if that name doesn't please you, we'll call it something else. We'll call it the person group. So they went along with us, and they trusted us, and that is partly my responsibility, because they thought, "These people wouldn't hurt us: the project coordinator is a Catholic." Rogers, however, was the principal investigator. . . . Rogers and I and eventually 58 others: we had 60 facilitators. We inundated that system with humanistic psychology. We called it Therapy for Normals, TFN. . . . We said, we'll help you look within. After all, is not God in your heart? Is it not sufficient to be yourself, and wouldn't that make you a good Catholic? And if it doesn't, then perhaps you shouldn't have been a Catholic in the first place. Well, after a while there weren't many Catholics left. . . .
>
> [Rogers] was the brains behind the project, and he was probably anti-Catholic; at the time I didn't recognize it because I probably was, too. We both had a bias against hierarchy. I was flush with Vatican II, and I thought, "I am the Church; I am as Catholic as the Pope.". . . We overcame their traditions, we overcame their faith.
>
> The IHMs had some 60 schools when we started; at the end, they had one. . . . There is no more Immaculate Heart College. It doesn't exist. It's ceased to function, because of our good offices. . . . There were some 615 nuns when we began. Within a year after our first interventions, 300 of them were petitioning Rome to get out of their vows. They did not want to be under anyone's authority, except the authority of their imperial inner selves. . . . It took about a year and a half [to destroy the Immaculate Heart Order]. We did similar programs for the Jesuits, for the Franciscans, for the Sisters of Providence, of Charity, and the Mercy Sisters. We did dozens of Catholic religious organizations. (Coulson 1994, 23)

The atheistic Abram Maslow was dumbfounded by this openness of Catholics to that which was antithetical to their faith. In a journal entry of 1962, Maslow wrote of his "successful lecture last night before hun-

dreds of Catholics. They shouldn't applaud me; they should attack. If
they knew what I was doing they would attack." (Coulson 1994, 20)

The scandals concerning the homosexual activity of priests with teenage
boys during the 1970s[1] are in part another result of secular psychology's
impact upon the Church.

> The proof of authenticity on the humanistic psychology model is to go
> against what you were trained to be, to call all of that phoniness, and to
> say what is deepest within you. What's deepest within you, however, are
> certain unrequited longings, including sexual longings. We provoked an
> epidemic of sexual misconduct among clergy and therapists. . . . Rogers
> got two honorary doctorates from Jesuit universities. They thought we
> were saviors. . . . [There] was a lot of talk about the "Third Way" among
> the Jesuits. The first two ways are faithful marriage and faithful celibacy.
> But now there was this more humane way, a more human way—all too
> human as I see it today. The idea was that priests could date. One priest,
> for example, defined his celibacy for me as, "It means I don't have to marry
> the girl" [It is now painfully apparent there was a *fourth*, even more
> unseemly way as well]. (Coulson 1994, 20)

Humanistic therapies such as Rogers's and Maslow's opened the lid of a
Pandora's box within the Church. From it spewed forth heresy and apostasy, as well as occult psychospirituality, feminism, and homosexuality that
subsequently metastasized within the ranks of the Church, especially the
religious orders. The campaign against the Holy Catholic Church was
given a weapon of mass destruction in the form of humanistic psychology.
Much of the urgency then for the establishment and promulgation of an
authentic Catholic clinical psychology stems from the grave need to witness against, undo the damage of, and supplant such schools as that of
Maslow and Rogers and their demonic psychospiritual spawns.

---

[1] For a further analysis of the Thomistic psychological dynamics of the clerical sexual sins of the 1970's see *Liturgical and Sexual Abuse* (Dilsaver, *Homiletic and Pastoral Review,* December 2007). See also *Articles,* www.IDPSY.com.

APPENDIX C

● ● ●

The Clinical Need for a Catholic Psychology

THE PHILOSOPHY of science speaks of the necessity of integrating the science of psychology (and science in general) into qualitative worldviews, while empirical studies recognize religiosity as a significant factor in psychological profiling. Although the reasoning employed in the preceding treatise is ultimately Thomistic, numerous modern authors from outside the Thomistic tradition have rediscovered the need for such integration.[1] Browning (1987) posited that science, and especially clinical psychology, cannot avoid a philosophical or metaphysical context. O'Donohue (1989) argued that a clinical psychologist must be not only a scientist and practitioner but a metaphysician as well. S. Jones (1996) built on O'Donohue's thesis and added "theologian," or at least to be "religion-literate," to the qualifications of a competent clinical psychologist. These writers combine with previous modern philosophers of science to advance a strong argument that science, and specifically psychology, is by itself unable or incompetent to provide or judge the metaphysical or philosophical, yet still depends on it for the fulfillment of its goals.

Beyond this general need of psychology to avail itself of qualitative worldviews, there is the need for psychology to avail itself of religion-specific worldviews. For over a century, empirical studies have indicated that the religiosity, and specifically Catholicity, of subjects significantly impacts their psychological profile, thus suggesting that religiosity is a pertinent factor in

---

[1] In accord with Thomism, chapter 2 delineates the inherent need the psychological sciences have of being integrated with, or, more strictly speaking, subalternated to, philosophy.

their treatment. Allport and Ross (1967) found that the type of religious orientation predicted ethnic prejudice: the devout ("intrinsically orientated") were found to be significantly less prejudiced than the less devout ("extrinsically orientated"). Batson and Ventis (1982) found that Allport's religious types predicted mental health, with intrinsic orientation being positively correlated and extrinsic being negatively correlated. Tate and Miller (1971) found that Allport's religious types corresponded with differing value systems. Kohn (1972) found that religiosity correlated highly with authoritarianism. Schwartz and Huismans (1995) found that across religions there is significant correlation between religiosity and values. Granqvist (2002) found evidence that insecurity and religious instability might be related.

Specifically in regard to Catholicity, Durkheim's (1897) seminal work on suicide found that Catholics were significantly less likely to commit suicide than Protestants, and concluded that some factor in Catholicism imparted an *immunity* to suicide. Some sixty-five years later, Dean and Reeves (1962) conducted a study that proximately supported Durkheim's findings by measuring levels of anomie (purposelessness) as an indicator of the general syndrome of alienation, which is an indicator of suicidal predisposition. This study found that women from a Catholic college scored significantly lower on anomie than did Protestant college women and that the Catholic women's scores decreased with each year of college, whereas the Protestant women's scores remained the same or rose. Knöpfelmacher and Armstrong (1963), as well as Stark (1971), found that Catholics were the only religious group whose high scores on authoritarianism did not positively correlate with a high score on ethnocentrism. In fact, Catholics scored the highest on authoritarianism but the lowest on ethnocentrism.[2] Fichter (1954) found that devout ("nuclear") Catholics showed significantly less ethnic prejudice than less devout Catholics. Maldonado Sierra, Trent, and Fernandez-Marina (1960) compared "neurotic" and "non-neurotic" subjects and found that those with traditional Catholic ("traditional Latin-American") family beliefs were significantly less neurotic than those who did not hold such beliefs.

---

[2] It is here hypothesized that this unique Catholic combination of high authoritarianism and low ethnocentricity is due to the unique nature of the Church herself: both to the fact that Catholic ecclesial authority is transpersonal—that is, it depends not on the person, but on the sacerdotal office—and to the fact that Catholicism is transcultural, being the only denomination that is truly catholic or universal.

However, new studies have not been as supportive of this significant difference. This is borne out, for instance, in a study of Catholics residing at senior citizen centers, who scored just minimally higher than their Protestant co-residents on purpose-in-life or anomie questionnaires (Gerwood, LeBlanc, and Piazza 1998). This is a striking divergence from the previously cited suicide study at the turn of the twentieth century and the study on college women just prior to Vatican II. This suggests that mainstream Catholicism no longer yields a significantly different psychological profile from the non-Catholic population. This is not surprising. Mainstream American Catholics no longer significantly differ from the general population on grave moral Catholic teachings either (for example, in regard to abortion, divorce, and contraception). Indeed, it is convincingly argued that Catholics are less a monolithic entity than perceived by the profession of psychology (Kehoe 1998). The lack of a significant Catholic profile is due to the secularization of Catholic cultures and subcultures, which in turn is due both to a general societal secularization and to intraecclesial secularization, which has occurred especially in the wake of the Second Vatican Council (1962–1965). (This author confidently hypothesizes that studying those devout pockets of populations that still integrally subscribe to the normative beliefs of Catholicism would render results comparable to the early studies.)

Finally, from a therapeutic perspective, the development of a Catholic clinical psychology is recommended. The profession of psychology has long recognized the need for therapists to factor in the religious worldview of therapants in order to treat them effectively. Such literature spans works from William James at the turn of the century to the present.[3] There is a strong professional appreciation of a therapant's subjective religious worldview as a factor in therapeutic alliance and effectiveness, as well as an issue of diversity sensitivity.

---

3 For instance, the American Psychological Association has in the last few years published three books on the importance of religiosity in therapy: *Religion and the Clinical Practice of Psychology*, ed. E. P. Shafranske (Washington, DC: American Psychological Association, 1996), *Integrating Spirituality into Treatment: Resources for Practitioners*, ed. W. R. Miller c1999. (Washington, DC: American Psychological Association, 1999), and *Handbook of Psychotherapy and Religious Diversity*, ed. P. S. Richards and A. E. Bergin (Washington, DC: American Psychological Association, 2000).

Glossary

Aggregate-Self: The existential individual all men experience upon self-reflection; it is body, pseudo-self, and imago Dei or authentic self.

Character: The enduring record of moral life that is formed by the habituation of virtue or vice.

Concupiscible Appetite: The emotional appetite attracted to that which gives sensible pleasure and repulsed by that which gives sensible pain. Concupiscible positive emotions are love, desire, and delight, and their respective contraries are the negative emotions of hate, flight, and loss.

Corresponding Continuums: Six corresponding continuums that conceptualize mental health in accord with the first, which is the typifying powers of the soul: *vegetative, sensitive,* and *rational.* The continuums then following in order: *openness-to-reality, cognition, volition, emotion,* and *clinical descriptors.* All the continuums are Thomistic conceptualizations save for the last, which correlates with classifications used by modern psychology.

Cupidity: Self-love; the unbridled desire for one's own pleasure, which along with its prerequisite, pride, is the root of all sin and the cause of the warping defense of personality.

Functional Materialism: The result of a person being to some degree fixated on material beings, where all the faculties of the soul are ordered toward fulfillment of a person's subjective material and emotional needs. Characteristic of Zone II.

Glee: The subjective experience of pleasure, marked by a feeling of pleased or satisfied gratification. The corollary of glee is sadness. Characteristic of Zone II.

Humiliation: If properly embraced, it is a psychological and spiritual mortification. If fought, it produces further secretions of "personality defense" as a protection for pride and self-love.

Imago Dei: Latin for "image of God," the authentic human person consisting of reason and volition. It is hidden by vice-necessitated personality and magnified by virtue. Its nemesis is the pseudo-self which seeks to supplant it.

Infantile Hedonism: The result of a person being fixated on his bodily and emotional sensations. This physical fixation can be seen as a regression in which a person is reduced to a primordial engagement with reality. Characteristic of Zone III.

Irascible Appetite: The emotional appetite inclined to overcome contraries and rise above obstacles in accord with the concupiscible appetite's desire or repugnance toward a thing. The irascible positive emotions are hope and audacity; their respective contraries despair and fear, as well as anger, which has no contrary, form the irascible negative emotions.

Joy: The objective experiencing of the goodness of life, which reaches its pinnacle in the Christian faith and is completely entailed in the resurrection of Jesus Christ. Joy is the corollary to sorrow. Characteristic of Zone I and beyond.

Persona: Social image, a necessary veneer that allows one to interact with people on a relatively superficial but functional level and is easily breached or discarded.

Personality: This is the result of vice's interaction with reality and thus is an apparatus of that which is vicious in the character.

Pietistic Persona: A pious mask that is presented to the outside world and to the community of believers and is to some degree inauthentic or in excess of the depths of a person's faith.

Powers and Faculties of the Soul: Thomists often use the terms powers and faculties interchangeably. For the sake of clarity IDP employs "powers" to refer to the larger tripartite abilities of the soul (vegetative, sensitive, and rational). "Faculties" refers to those more specific abilities of the soul that Aquinas discovered as emanating from one of the tripartite powers, especially those facilities that emanate from the rational power.

Pride: The lack of submission to God, that, with its necessary corollary cupidity or inordinate self-love, is the root of all sin and the cause of the warping defense of personality.

Pseudo-self: The false-self that is comprised of pride and self-love that one must die to in order to manifest his imago Dei.

Psychic Mortification: The process of embracing humiliation. It is the highest form of mortification and entails the psychological and spiritual mortification of dying to self-love and pride.

Psychological Mortification: A form of psychic mortification. The process in which a person embraces and even facilitates the humiliations inherent in his life and thus allows his personality defenses to be breeched and pride and self-love to be diminished.

Psychovitiation: The iatrogenic (induced inadvertently) psychological intervention that exacerbates or creates mental illness.

Reality: Used both commonly and specifically in IDP to refer to the precognitive or existential encountering of being-as-such.

(The) Real: The term is used in IDP's formal definitions to refer to all aspects of being which distinguishes it from IDP's specific technical use of the term "reality".

Reflection, Reflecting upon: In IDP these terms refer to the Thomistic process of judgment.

Receptive Humiliation: Humiliation that is part and parcel of one's existence and imposed from outside a person's control.

Reflective Humiliation: Humiliation that is generated by a person's own cognition and thus self-imposed and under his control.

Sadness: Self-pity that arises from a person's self-love, pride, and subjective appraisal of suffering. Characteristic of Zone II.

Sorrow: The objective experiencing of the suffering of human life, which reaches its pinnacle in the Christian faith and is completely entailed in the crucifixion of Jesus Christ. Sorrow is the corollary of joy. Characteristic of Zone I and beyond.

Spiritual Mortification: A form of psychic mortification. The highest form of mortification, in which God's presence is withdrawn from the senses. This process is fully manifest in the rare phenomenon of the "dark night of the soul." Spiritual mortification can be seen as the apex of humiliation, where the elect are called to completely die to self and purge themselves of all self-love that may be concomitant in their love of God.

Suffering: Experiencing the negative aspects of existence. It can be experienced as pain, sadness, or sorrow.

Therapant: An IDP designation that connotes an active participation in the therapeutic process and avoids the passive connotations of *patient* and the consumeristic connotations of *client.*

Therapeutic Humiliation: A controlled and measured humiliation imposed in a therapeutic manner by the IDP psychotherapist.

Visceral Emotions: The designation when the objects of the emotions are primarily physical sensation. Visceral emotions are equivalent to the estimative emotions of nonrational animals. A person who is fixated on visceral emotions is dominated by physical *pain* and *pleasure.* Characteristic of Zone III.

Bibliography

Allers, R. 1933. *The New Psychologies*. London and New York: Sheed and Ward.

———. 1934. *The Psychology of Character*. New York: Sheed and Ward.

———. 1940. *The Successful Error: A Critical Study of Freudian Psychology*. New York: Sheed and Ward.

Allport, G. W., and Ross, J. M. 1967. "Personal Religious Orientation and Prejudice." *Journal of Personality and Social Psychology* 5, no. 4:432–43.

Altham, E. 1999. "The Religion of the Self: An Interview with Dr. William Coulson." *Latin Mass Magazine* 8:4.

American Psychiatric Association. 2000. *Diagnostic and Statistical Manual of Mental Disorders*. 4th ed. rev. Washington, DC: Author.

American Psychological Association. 2002a. *About the American Psychological Association: What Is Psychology?* Retrieved from www.apa.org/about.

———. 2002b. APA Bylaws. Retrieved from www.apa.org/governance/bylaws/art1.html.

Aristotle. 1984. *The Complete Works of Aristotle*. Princeton: Princeton University Press.

Attwater, D. A. 1961. *A Catholic Dictionary*. New York: Macmillan Company.

Augustine. 1993. *On the Free Choice of the Will*. Trans. T. Williams. Cambridge: Hackett Publishing.

Balthasar, H. U. 2000. *The Christian and Anxiety*. San Francisco: Ignatius Press.

Batson, C. D., and L. W. Ventis. 1982. "Consequences of the Religious Experience: Mental Health or Sickness?" In *The Religious Experience: A Social Psychological Perspective*, 7, 211–51. New York: Oxford University Press.

Bittle, C. N. 1945. *The Whole Man: Psychology*. Milwaukee: Bruce Publishing.

Brennan, R. E. 1941. *Thomistic Psychology*. New York: Macmillan.

———. 1952. *General Psychology: A Study of Man Based on St. Thomas Aquinas*. Rev. ed. New York: Macmillan.

Browning, D. S. 1987. *Religious Thought and the Modern Psychologies.* Philadelphia: Fortress.

Callahan, G. 2002. "What Is Science?" www.lewrockwell.com/callahan/callahan92.html

Cooper, J. E., et al. 1972. *Psychiatric Diagnosis in New York and London.* New York: Oxford University Press.

Coulson, W. 1994. "Repentant Psychologist: How I Wrecked the I.H.M. Nuns." *The Latin Mass: A Chronicle of Catholic Reform* (Special Edition). Fort Collins: Roman Catholic Books.

Dean, D. G., and J. A. Reeves. 1962. "Anomie: A Comparison of a Catholic and a Protestant Sample. *Sociometry* 25:209–12.

De Chivré, B.-M. 1995. *Garnets Spirituels,* No. 1. Controverses: Bulle, 1995. Translated by Angelus Press in *The Angelus* 27, no. 12 (December 2004).

Decrees of the Council of Trent. 1978. Trans. H. J. Schroeder. Rockford, IL: Tan Books.

De Finance, J. 1991. *An Ethical Inquiry.* Rome: Editrice Pontificia Università Gregoriana.

Denzinger, H. 1962. *Enchiridion Symbolorum.* Barcelona: Herder.

Dilsaver, Grover C. 1954. The administrative assistant in the elementary schools of the Montebello Unified School District. M.S. thesis, University of Southern California School of Education.

Dilsaver, G. C. 1997. *Scepter, Crosier, and Cross: The Call to Christian Patriarchy.* Portions published in *Christian Order* 42, no. 12:648–60, and 43, no. 6/7:413–24.

———. 2001. "A Story of the Soul." *Catholic Faith* 7, no. 5:29–32.

———. 2003. The placeholder of secularity to ensure scientific integrity and worldview diversity in the profession of psychology. Paper presented at the Mid-Winter Meeting of the American Psychological Association's Division 36, Baltimore, MD.

———. 2007, December. "Liturgical and Sexual Abuse." *Homiletic and Pastoral Review.*

Durkheim, E. 1897. "Egoistic Suicide." *Suicide,* 152–216. Toronto: Free Press.

Fichter, J. H. 1954. *Social Relations in the Urban Parish.* Chicago: University of Chicago Press.

Francis, L. J., and C. F. J. Ross. 2000. "Personality Type and the Quest Orientation of Religiosity." *Journal of Psychological Type* 55:12–25.

Gerwood, J. B., M. LeBlanc, and N. Piazza. 1998. "The Purpose-in-Life Test and Religious Denomination: Protestant and Catholic Scores in an Elderly Population." *Journal of Clinical Psychology* 54:49–53.

Gillespie, C. K. 2001. *Psychology and American Catholicism.* New York: Crossroad Publishing.

Gilson, E. 1956. *Introduction to Thomas Aquinas.* New York: Random.

———. 1960. *Elements of Christian Philosophy.* Garden City, NY: Doubleday.

Goethe, J. W. 1988. *Goethe: The Collected Works.* Vol. 12, *Scientific Studies.* Ed. and trans. D. Miller. Princeton, NJ: Princeton University Press.

Granqvist, P. 2002. "Attachment and Religiosity in Adolescence: Cross-Sectional and Longitudinal Evaluations." *Personality and Social Psychology Bulletin* 28, no. 2:260–70.

Hardon, J. A., 2002. "The Meaning of Virtue in Thomas Aquinas." Retrieved from www.intermirifica.org/thaquinas.htm. Taken from *Great Catholic Books Newsletter* 2, no. 1.

Hathaway, W. L. 2001a. "Clinical Sciences and Clinical Epistemologies: Internalist Versus Externalist Accounts." Paper presented at the annual convention of the American Psychological Association, San Francisco, CA.

———. 2001b. "Worldviews and Integration." Unpublished lecture: Regent University, Virginia Beach, VA.

———. (2003). "Impairment in Religious Functioning as a Clinically Significant Assessment Issue." *Mental Health, Religion, & Culture,* Vol. 6, no. 2, 2003.

Hempel, C. G. 1965. *Aspects of Scientific Explanation and Other Essays in the Philosophy of Science.* New York: Free Press.

Hergermann, C. G., ed. 1911. *The Catholic Encyclopedia: An International Work of Reference of the Constitution, Doctrine, Discipline, and History of the Catholic Church.* New York: Robert Appleton.

James, W. 1882, republished in 1999. *The Varieties of Religious Experience.* New York: Random House.

John Paul II. 1991, May 1 Encyclical Letter: *Centesimus Annus* (46). Rome: St. Peter's.

———. 1992, May–June. "Moral Responsibility of Psychiatrists." *The Pope Speaks,* 178–79.

———. 1998, September 14. Encyclical Letter: *Fides et Ratio* (43, 44).

Jones, E. M. 2000. *Libido Dominandi: Sexual Liberation and Political Control.* South Bend, IN: St. Augustine's Press.

Jones, S. 1996. "A Constructive Relationship for Religion with the Science and Profession of Psychology: Perhaps the Boldest Model Yet." In *Handbook of Religion and the Clinical Practice of Psychology,* ed. E. P. Shafranske, 113–47. Washington, DC: American Psychological Association.

Kehoe, N. C. 1998. "Religion and Mental Health from the Catholic Perspective." In *Handbook of Religion and Mental Health,* ed. H. G. Koenig, 212–23. San Diego: Academic Press.

Kilpatrick, W. K. 1983. *Psychological Seduction: The Failure of Modern Psychology.* Nashville: Thomas Nelson Publishers.

Kimball, R. 2000. "Notes and Comments: Science and Nature." *New Criterion* 18, no. 8.

Kinsella, N. 1960. *Unprofitable Servants: Conferences on Humility.* Dublin: M. H. Gill and Son,

Knöpfelmacher, F., and D. B. Armstrong. 1963. "The Relation Between Authoritarianism, Ethnocentrism and Religious Denominations Among Australian Adolescence." *American Catholic Sociological Review* 24:99–114.

Kohn, P. M. 1972. "The Authoritarianism-Rebellion Scale: A Balanced F Scale with Left-wing Reversals." *Sociometry* 35:176–89.

Lambert, M. J. 1992. "Psychotherapy Outcome Research: Implications for Integrative and Eclectic Therapists." In *Handbook of Psychotherapy Integration*, ed. J. C. Norcross and M. R. Goldfried, 94–29. New York: Basic Books.

Leo XIII. 1879, August 4. Encyclical Letter: *Aeterni Patris* (18).

Lindworsky, J. 1931. *Experimental Psychology.* New York: Macmillan.

———. 1932. *Theoretical Psychology.* St. Louis: Herder.

———. 1932. *The Training of the Will* (reprint). Ft. Collins, CO: Roman Catholic Books.

Magner, J. 1953. *Mental Health in a Mad World.* Milwaukee: Bruce Publishing Company.

Maher, M. 1930. *Psychology: Empirical and Rational.* 9th ed. New York: Longmans, Green.

Maldonado Sierra, E. D., R. D. Trent, and R. Fernandez Marina. 1960. "Neurosis and Traditional Family Beliefs in Puerto Rico." *International Journal of Social Psychiatry* 6:237–46.

Marcel, G. 1956. *The Philosophy of Existentialism.* New York: Citadel Press.

Maturin, B. W. 1939. *Self-knowledge and Self-discipline.* Patterson, NJ: St. Anthony Guild Press.

Maxmen, J. S. and N. G. Ward. 1995. *Essential Psychopathology and Its Treatment.* 2nd ed. rev. New York: W. W. Norton.

May, R., E. Angel, and H. F. Ellenberger, eds. 1958. *Existence: A New Dimension in Psychiatry and Psychology.* New York: Basic Books.

Miller, W. R., ed. 1999. *Integrating Spirituality into Treatment: Resources for Practitioners.* Washington, DC: American Psychological Association.

Misiak, H., and V. M. Staudt. 1954. *Catholics in Psychology: A Historical Survey.* New York: McGraw-Hill.

Müller, J. 1834. *Handbuch der Physiologie des Menschen für Verkesungen.* Coblenz: J. Hölscher.

Newman, J. H. 1906. *Discourses Addressed to Mixed Congregations.* London: Longmans, Green.

O'Donohue, W. 1989. "The (Even) Bolder Model: The Clinician as Metaphysician-Scientist-Practitioner." *American Psychologist* 44:1460–68.

Pascal, B. 1660. *Pensées,* trans. A. J. Krailsheimer. London: Penguin Books, 1966.

Pacwa, M. 1992. *Catholics and the New Age.* Ann Arbor, MI: Servant Publications.

Peterson, R., et al. 1997. "The National Council of Schools and Programs of Professional Psychology Educational Model." *Professional Psychology: Research and Practice* 28, no. 4:373–86.

Pieper, J. 1991. *Guide to Thomas Aquinas.* San Francisco: Ignatius Press; translation, New York: Pantheon Books, 1962.

———. 1989. *Living the Truth* (reprint). San Francisco: Ignatius Press.

Pius X. 1907, July 3. *Lamentabili Sane.* Vatican: Notary of the Holy Roman and Universal Inquisition.

———. 1907, September 8. Encyclical Letter: *Pascendi Dominici Gregis.* Rome: St. Peter's.

Pius XII. 1953, April 13. *Address to the Fifth International Congress on Psychotherapy and Clinical Psychology* (40). Rome: Vatican.

———. 1958, April 10. *Address to the Rome Congress of the International Association of Applied Psychology* (112). Rome: Vatican.

Putney, S., and R. Middleton. 1961. "Rebellion, Conformity, and Parental Religious Ideologies. *Sociometry* 24, no. 2:125–35.

Reinhardt, K. F. 1952. *The Existentialist Revolt: The Main Themes and Phases of Existentialism.* Milwaukee: Bruce Publishing.

Richards, P. S., and A. E. Bergin, eds. 2000. *Handbook on Psychotherapy and Religious Diversity.* Washington, DC: American Psychological Association.

Ripperger, C. 2000. *Introduction to the Science of Mental Health.* Vol. 1–3. Self-published.

Robinson, D. N. 1995. *An Intellectual History of Psychology.* 3rd ed. Madison: University of Wisconsin Press.

———, speaker. 1999. *The Great Ideas of Psychology: Foundations and Psychology in the Empiricist Tradition.* Cassette Course Number 660, part 1. Chantilly, VA: Teaching Company.

Rupp, J. 2000. *Prayers to Sophia.* Philadelphia: Innisfree.

Schwartz, S. H., and L. Sagiv. 1995. "Identifying Cultural-specifics in the Content and Structure of Values." *Journal of Cross-Cultural Psychology* 26:92–116.

Schwartz, S. H., and S. Huismans. 1995. "Value Priorities and Religiosity in Four Western Religions." *Social Psychology Quarterly* 58, no. 2:88–107.

Shafranske, Edward P., ed. 1996. *Religion and the Clinical Practice of Psychology.* Washington, DC: American Psychological Association.

Sheen, F. J. 1938. *God and Intelligence in Modern Philosophy: A Critical Study in the Light of the Philosophy of Saint Thomas.* London: Longmans, Green.

———. 1951. *Peace of Soul* (reprint). Garden City, NY: Garden City Books.

Smith, W. 1993. "Questions Answered." *Homiletic and Pastoral Review.* March edition.

Soloviev, V. 1915. *War, Progress and the End of History, Including a Short Story of the Anti-Christ: Three Discussions by Vladimir Soloviev.* Trans. A. Bakshy. London: University of London Press.

Stark, R. 1971. "Psychopathology and Religious Commitment." *Review of Religious Research* 12:165–76.

Tanquerey, A. D. 1959. *A Manual of Dogmatic Theology.* Trans. J. J. Byrnes. New York: Desclee.

Tate, E. D., and G. R. Miller. 1971. "Differences in Value Systems of Persons with Varying Religious Orientations." *Journal for the Scientific Study of Religion* 10:357–65.

Thomas à Kempis. 1976. *The Imitation of Christ.* New York: Doubleday.

Thomas Aquinas. 1947. *Theologiae: First Complete American Edition in Three Volumes.* Trans. Fathers of the English Dominican Province. New York: Benzinger Brothers.

Unamuno, Miguel de. 1905. *Selected Works of Miguel de Unamuno: Our Lord Don Quixote.* Vol. 3, ed. Anthony Kerrigan and Martin Nozick, trans. Anthony Kerrigan 1967. Bollingen Series 85. Princeton: Princeton University Press.

U.S. Religious Landscape Survey, The Pew Forum on Religion and Public Life (2008) retrieved from religions.pewforum.org/reports

Vanderveldt, J. H., and R. P. Odenwald. 1952. *Psychiatry and Catholicism.* New York: McGraw-Hill.

Van Kaam, A. 1966. *Existential Counseling.* Wilkes-Barres, PA: Dimension Books.

Vitz, P. C. 1977. *Psychology as Religion: The Cult of Self-worship.* Grand Rapids, MI: William B. Eerdmans Publishing.

Walters, B. W. 2001. *Children and Behavior: Faith and Psychiatry. Latin Mass* 10, no. 2:72–73.

Weigert, A. J., and D. L. Thomas. 1970. "Socialization and Religiosity: A Cross-national Analysis of Catholic Adolescents. *Sociometry* 33, no. 3:305–26.

Yalom, I. D. 1980. *Existential psychotherapy.* New York: Basic Books.

Index

Socrates, 76
Socratic method, 127
Soloviev, Vladimir, 166
sorrow-joy (marshaled emotionality),
    116, 138, 139, 140, 141–42, 182,
    183
soul and brain, hylomorphism of,
    28–29, 43–46
spiritual elements of IDP, 153–68. *See
    also* original sin; sin
    communality, importance of,
        161–63
    Dasein-in-Christ therapeutic
        relationship, 82, 159–61
    existentialism as religious matter,
        163–64
    faith and reason, relationship
        between, 33–35, 154–57,
        163–65
    God, existence of, 35*n*5, 69,
        153–55
    openness-to-reality, 102–3,
        158–59, 164–65
    pietistic persona, 154, 157, 182
    Virgin Mary as pattern of
        psychological health, 166–68
Spiritual Exercises of St. Ignatius of
    Loyola, 10
spiritual health, 102–3, 158–59,
    164–65
spiritual mortification, 147, 183
spiritual pride, 117
Stark, R., 178
Staudt, V. M., 14–16
stoicism, 38*n*7
striving-for-the-good in the Moral
    Agency Schema, 121–24, 129–32
Stumpf, Carl, 3

subalternation
    of IDP to Catholic theology, xv–xvi,
        26–27
    of psychology to philosophy, 28–30
subjectivism
    authentic self transcending, 109–10
    of Descartes, 63
    as epistemological distortion, 55
    humanistic psychology
        encouraging, 69, 110
    IDP's coupling with objective
        metaphysics, 68–69
subsidiarity, 163
substance abuse, 97
Suenens, Leo Cardinal, 9–10
suffering
    defined, 184
    hatred of personality and vicious
        elements of self, developing, 142
    personality, IDP's theory of, 109,
        110, 111–13, 142–43
    physical mortification or volitional
        suffering, 142–44
    as therapeutic mechanism, 138
    therapeutic mechanism, suffering-
        well as, 150–51
    of Virgin Mary, 167
suicide
    Catholicism and risk of, 178–79
    existentialism and, 75–76
    nihilism and rise of, 56
symptomology, 94–95
synderesis (primordial conscience),
    122, 123, 124, 129, 131

Tanquerey, A. D., 44, 154*n*2
Tate, E. D., 178
teleology of IDP, 37–38
    existential teleology, 71–72

tripartite conceptualization of mental
health, 85–103, 171
  corresponding continuums with
    typifying powers, 86, 87, 181.
    See also clinical descriptors;
    cognition; emotions or passions;
    openness-to-reality; volition
  faculties or powers of the soul,
    86*n*2, 182
  spiritual health differentiated from
    mental health, 102–3
  Zone I (rational power), 85, 87,
    100–101, 141
  Zone II (sensitive power), 85, 87,
    98–99, 139
  Zone III (vegetative power), 85, 87,
    95–97, 139
truth
  being in mode of truth when
    engaged cognitively, 120–21
  centrality of, 60–62
  convincing (pedagogy of truth),
    126–27
  good, relationship to, 57
  knowability of, 53–54
  sight-of-the-truth in the Moral
    Agency Schema, 121–24,
    126–30
  suffering and, 111–12
  synonymity of reality, being, truth,
    and good, 60–61, 70–71, 91–92

Ultimate Concerns of secular
  existentialism, 71, 73–74
Unamuno, Miguel de, 130
unity with God, 83
utilitarianism, 83

Van Kaam, Adrian, 8, 81
Vanderveldt, James H., 4
Vatican I, 153*n*1
Vatican II, 9–11, 174, 179
Vatican pronouncements on
  psychology, 2, 5, 11, 13–14. *See also*
  individual popes, e.g. John Paul II
vegetative power (Zone III), 85, 87,
  95–97, 139
Ventis, L. W., 178
vice
  anxiety, vicious, 78, 79, 80
  character formed by habituation of,
    106
  defined, 127
  hatred of personality and vicious
    elements of self, developing, 142
  pride as root of, 145
  truth, impaired sight of, 127–28
vice-effects, 127–28
Vienna, Council of, 44*n*14
Virgin Mary, 166–68
virtue
  anxiety, virtuous, 78, 79–80
  character formed by habituation of,
    106
  humility as basis of, 145
  intellectual virtues, 101
visceral emotionality (pain-pleasure),
  115–16, 138, 139, 140, 143, 144,
  184
Vitz, Paul, 11
volition
  being in mode of the good when
    engaged volitionally, 121
  existentialist focus on, 74
  as moral act, 91
  Moral Agency Schema, steps in,
    122–24

● ● ●

Legal and Clinical Training Notices

ONLY CERTIFIED Imago Dei Psychotherapy psychotherapists may claim to use Imago Dei Psychotherapy or Imago Dei Psychotherapy psychotherapeutic techniques. Certification is open to psychologists, psychiatrists, and master level clinicians. The Imago Dei Psychotherapy certification process entails academic training in theology, spirituality, philosophy and psychotherapy. In addition, clinicians in training must undergo Imago Dei Psychotherapy as a therapant and have a portion of their clinical casework supervised. Please visit IDPSY.COM for further information.